...Iorthampton, Mass.

...nd engraved by S.E. Brown.

...s in the center of the engraving.

BID US GOD SPEED

BID US GOD SPEED

*The History of the Edwards Church
Northampton, Massachusetts
1833 / 1983*

by

Ruth E. and C. Keith Wilbur

Published for the
EDWARDS CHURCH OF NORTHAMPTON
by
PHOENIX PUBLISHING
Canaan, New Hampshire

BX
7255
.N85
E325
1983

> Wilbur, Ruth E.
>   Bid us God speed.
>
>   Includes index.
>   1. Edwards Church (Northampton, Mass.) I. Wilbur,
> C. Keith, 1923-   II. Title.
> BX7255.N85E325   1983   285.8'74423   82-22347
> ISBN 0-914016-93-8

Copyright 1983 by Ruth E. and C. Keith Wilbur

All rights reserved. No part of this publication may be reproduced, stored in a retrieval system or transmitted in any form or by any means without the prior written permission of the publisher, except for brief quotations in a review.

Printed in the United States of America
by Courier Printing Company
Binding by New Hampshire Bindery
Design by A. L. Morris

CONTENTS

Foreword		vii
1833-1836	John Todd / Birthing of a New Church	1
1836-1842	John Mitchell / A Growing Congregation	8
1843-1846	E. P. Rogers / A Personality in the Pulpit	10
1848-1851	George E. Day / Reforms and Christian Ideals	11
1852-1879	Gordon Hall / Building a New Church	13
1882-1891	Isaac Clark / Emphasis on Sabbath School Education	19
1892-1898	Paul Van Dyke / Something for Everyone	23
1899-1902	Peter McMillan / "The Trenda" Success	24
1903-1912	Willis H. Butler / 75th Birthday Celebration	26
1913-1918	Irving Maurer / Impact of Reforms	27
1919-1928	Kenneth B. Welles / Pride in President Coolidge	31
1928-1931	James N. Armstrong / Continued Growth	33
1932-1939	Albert J. Penner / Our 100th Anniversary	34
1939-1945	Paul T. McClurkin / World War II Problems	39
1945-1954	L. Byron Whipple / Sprucing up the Old Church	42
1954-1960	Richard Linde / Building the Present Church	48
1960-1975	Richard K. Beebe / The Ecumenical Movement	59
1975-1979	J. Gregory Tweed / Family Participation and Local Concerns	66
1979-	Anthony E. Acheson / A Church for All Ages	69
Edwards Church Family Album		73
Illustrations and Credits		90
Index		91

"Many of the customs and beliefs that sum up
'The American Way of Life' are the product of the New England
religious experiment known as the Congregational Way.
For this tradition, if for nothing else, every living American
is in debt to the first settlers of Massachusetts.
The Pilgrims and Puritans gave us not only Congregationalism,
but also Thanksgiving, the town meeting, our first university,
our first coeducational college, public schools and Mother
Goose. They started the Revolution (the Minute Men at
Lexington and Concord were Congregationalists almost to a
man). They brought the civil liberties of England's Magna
Charta to the American continent. They helped develop
in America the system of free enterprise.
More intangibly, the Puritans bestowed upon the American
spirit a dogged reliance on Providence, a faith in our ability to
win over any odds, a restlessness and inability to settle down,
a humility before God and, at the same time, a vaulting
egoism that refuses to admit any human authority as our master.
These characteristics are stamped on the American personality;
they were impressed there by the Puritans."

HARTZELL SPENCE
"The Congregationalists," Look Magazine, Dec. 8, 1959

"To most citizens of Northampton, Jonathan Edwards is either
a shadowy figure of antiquity, an earlier townsman whose name
is kept alive by the city's two Congregational churches, or else
he is remembered as a preacher of fire and brimstone who
painted the agonies of sinners writhing in the hands of an angry God.
Nevertheless it is important to remind ourselves that from
1729 to 1748 the profoundest thinker in 18th century America
devoted his talents and energy to the edification of 600
parishioners in an isolated river town. Many distinguished men
and women have been identified with Northampton since the
days when Edwards preached, but he still remains her
preeminent genius—a restlessly speculative scientist, an acute
psychologist, a world-famous theologian and philosopher."

DANIEL AARON
"Jonathan Edwards," The Northampton Book 1954

FOREWORD

FOR SOME REASON or other, churches are referred to as female—"her" spire—"she" stands on the corner of State and Main Streets—the "daughter" of old First church. Certainly the women of Edwards have championed innumerable causes these 150 years—fairs, missions, Sunday school teaching, church dinners, the Edwards Shop, to name but a few, and have been prime movers in the many reform movements throughout our history. As for a "he" church, our 19 ministers have all been men, and the male members have admirably answered the call for fundraising, planning, and church maintenance (although their attendance has occasionally been a sometimes thing). Our Sunday school is filled with *both* boys and girls, the pride of the congregation and the hope for our church in the future.

Perhaps, if it weren't so awkward, Edwards should be called the "us" church. Regardless of gender, age differences, financial where-with-all, race or color—WE are the church. The Edwards Church family continues to contribute its combined talents and energies to further the glory of God. In our congregational and therefore democratic way of life, the opinions, enthusiasm, and contributions of the individual make the direction of our church all the more meaningful. In using "her" or "she" when referring to Edwards, the meaning is really the "everyone" place of worship.

The congregational spirit and the tradition of Jonathan Edwards have thrived in the Edwards Church family. Certainly the credit must go to the dedicated parishioners and guiding pastors who have met together these past 150 years. All should be mentioned in some detail, but such is not the case. Several volumes would be needed to do so. Therefore, to the many who shaped Edwards Church's history through the decades but who remain unnamed, this anniversary book is dedicated.

Ruth E. and C. Keith Wilbur

Northampton, Massachusetts
August 15, 1982

BID US
GOD SPEED

1833-1836

John Todd

Birthing of a New Church

IT WAS A FRIGID day in January when the westbound stagecoach clattered over the great bridge that spanned the Connecticut River. Once on the Northampton side, the driver gave the customary blast on his trumpet to announce the stage's arrival. It did not exactly match Gabriel's in quality, but to one passenger it gave notice that he was in Jonathan Edwards's country. Here was the town that sparked the Great Awakening nearly one hundred years before—a no-nonsense return to the basics of Congregational beliefs. The passenger, the Reverend John Todd, thought it fitting that his new pastorate should be named after that great theologian.

The yellow stage rumbled past the tidy white homes on Bridge Street, framed by the purplish, snow-covered humps of Mount Tom and Mount Holyoke. Here lived his parishioners—a courageous, dedicated lot. Just 99 in number, they had separated from the venerable old First Church, and they had no meetinghouse, no "Articles of Practice," and little else but enthusiasm. Ahead was Northampton's wide Main Street with busy shops that offered everything from books and dry goods to hardware and groceries. Perhaps his $1,000 yearly salary would stretch enough for him to be able to buy some of these essentials. Standing on the right side of the street, was the magnificent First Church, the pride of the town. It dominated the entire streetscape.

Mr. Todd had earlier written his concerns to the Edwards Society committee about separating from this parent church. "Do they feel kindly to you? Do they bid you God-speed, or have they feelings of jealousy?" He had been reassured by the answer. In the previous year, 1832, the church was bulging with 728 members and a parish of 2,800 souls, straining the energies and resources of the present minister beyond any reasonable limit. The separation proposal of 31 petitioners offered a solution.

The Undersigned, members of this Church, with serious and prayerful consideration, having taken some measures preliminary to the forming of a new Church and Society in this town, respectfully represent to our Christian Brethren, the hope [that they will] extend to us the hand of fellowship and bid us 'God speed'. It is not our object to form a party—or to create a division of interests among our brethren. We seek only to further the cause of Christ, and to enlarge the borders of His kingdom.

To Mr. Todd's relief, the separation was with the blessing of the mother church which replied in a letter that the action was "for the good of souls in this town."

The bone-rattling journey from Todd's former pastorate of Groton—hard by Lowell—was over at last. Another sounding of the driver's trumpet emphasized the arrival at the Warner's Tavern stage stop. No doubt the Edwards Society parishioners were there to greet the newcomer. Just as likely, they ushered him into the two-storied landmark. One could drive out the January chill from one's bones before two roaring fires in the parlors. For this group, however, there would be none of the inner warmth that flowed freely in the Tavern's barroom.

The townspeople now could size up this pastor, as a New Englander would do upon meeting any stranger. He was described as a large-framed Vermonter, with his "hair bristling and stiff—perpendicular, horizontal every way but downwards, his head in its own contour looking not a little like the Charter Oak, with its branches scraggy and defiant." As for the man himself, he was later said to "have a mind like a Corliss steam engine—and moving any number of wheels." Here was a real go-getter, ready to roll up his sleeves and make the Edwards Society more than just a name.

The wheels of that steam engine were moving rapidly. On January 30, 1833, a double ceremony marked the formal installation of its pastor. Mr. Todd presented the Articles of Faith and Covenant. There were twenty basic "standing rules," including number 12: "All male members who are heads of families, shall regularly and daily maintain family worship." Number 16 stated that "admonition and excommunication are to be administered

Bid Us God Speed

> ## TO THE MEMBERS OF THE FIRST CHURCH IN NORTHAMPTON.
>
> CHRISTIAN FRIENDS—
>
> The Undersigned, members of this Church, with serious and prayerful consideration, having taken some measures preliminary to the forming of a new Church and Society in this town—respectfully represent to our Christian Brethren, the hope, that a brief statement of our reasons for so doing, will not only remove any unpleasant impressions which may exist in relation to our undertaking, but will induce them still to extend to us the hand of fellowship, and bid us "God speed."
>
> It is *not* our object to *form a party*—or to create a division of interests among our brethren ; we seek only to further the cause of Christ, and to enlarge the borders of his kingdom ; and if it shall appear to our brethren, that by the course we are pursuing, the cause of pure religion will be advanced, we are confident the hope of securing their approbation will not be vain.
>
> There are *many* and *weighty* reasons for our believing that the formation of a new Church and Society is expedient. *First*—The extent of our parish. In 1831, its population was about 2800 souls—a larger number, probably, than is contained in any other society in this, or any of the New England States.
>
> Now it is well known that 1000 to 1500 persons, have *ever* been considered as large a number as could properly be supplied by the labours of one Clergyman ; and it is well known also, that much more labour is expected of Ministers at the present day, than was, twenty, or ten years since.
>
> If these positions are correct, (and we think they are,) our parish affords ample field for the labours of *two active, faithful Ministers of the Gospel*. And that one man is utterly inadequate to supply the spiritual wants of this great people, is both proved by the experience, and expressed by the opinions of our late pastors, Mr. Spencer and Mr. Tucker. We think their opinions worthy of consideration.
>
> Again—The population of the town is continually increasing. In 1820, we had 2854 inhabitants ; in 1830, 3613—making an increase in ten years of 759. Now it is generally admitted that the prospect of an increase of population was as good in 1830, as it was in 1820, and if the event shall prove this opinion correct, in 1840, less than eight years hence, we shall number 4573—960 more than in 1830. The increase of our parish in the same time, if it be in ratio equal to that of the whole town, will be about 700.
>
> How, we would ask, is this additional population to be provided with the ordinances of the Gospel? Can they be crowded into our already overflowing house ; and if they could, would you *add* them to the charge of one man who had already 2800 souls entrusted to his care? *We* believe their spiritual wants can in no way be met so well, as by the formation of another Church and Society.
>
> Again—We are of the opinion, that *now* is the *most favourable* time, that *nothing* is to be *gained*, while *much* may be *lost* by delay. The readiness of various individuals to go forward in the accomplishment of this object, is a consideration too important to be lost sight of, and as we are now destitute of the services of an active pastor, those attachments which ever exist between the faithful minister and his people, will not operate to divert us from the path of duty.
>
> We are well aware that there are many and great obstacles to be overcome,—aside from the large pecuniary sacrifice we shall have to make, it will demand no small share of resolution to leave so large a part of our christian brethren—to vacate our seats in the house where most of us have worshipped God from our childhood—to go out to form other friendships—and to look out another place of worship. In *addition to these*, must we be called to meet the frowns and disapprobation of our brethren—to sacrifice the friendship and good feeling that have so long existed between us? We hope not. For *other* sacrifices we have felt prepared—for *this —we have not*. Our appeal is to our brethren—to those with whom we have so often sat beneath the droppings of the Sanctuary—will *they* hedge up our path?—To those with whom we have sat around the table of Him, "whose banner over us was *love*," while afresh we pledged our all to promote his cause— will *they* dissuade us— will *they* erect the only insurmountable barrier, and thus neutralize our efforts and disappoint our hopes? We think not.
>
> Our appeal is to our brethren—shall it be in vain?
>
> May we not rather hope that the reasons which have influenced us to enlist in this enterprize, will induce others also—especially from among our elder brethren—to cast in their lot with us, and afford us that counsel which wisdom and experience will enable them to give, and which is so necessary to the success of our undertaking.
>
> | | | |
> |---|---|---|
> | ENOCH JEWETT. | AMANDA WOOD. | DANIEL BUTLER, JR. |
> | ZENAS WRIGHT. | EDWIN SPOONER. | J. P. WILLISTON. |
> | JOHN PHILLIPS. | ERASTUS SLATE. | ANSEL ABELS. |
> | EPHRAIM CUSHMAN. | ROBERT CROSSETT, JR. | ARIEL RANKIN. |
> | AARON BRECK. | CHAUNCEY COLTON. | M. T. MOODY. |
> | WM. CLARK, JR. | SETH STRONG. | W. H. STODDARD. |
> | MOSES BRECK. | BENJ. E. COOK. | ANSEL JEWETT. |
> | ELIHU CLARK. | ASAHEL S. ABELS. | LYMAN PARSONS |
> | JARED CLARK. | DANIEL R. CLARK. | THOMAS BRIDGMAN. |
> | JABEZ FRENCH. | EDWARD H. LITTLE. | JOHN BRIDGMAN |
> | ISAAC BRIDGMAN. | | |

Broadside addressed to congregation of the First Church in 1832.

by the Pastor." Number 19 went on to say that members are expected to refrain from selling or using "ardent spirits"—the stamp of "a doubtful Christian character."

With the guidelines in order, the Society was on its way. In his diary, the new minister recorded that "almost all of my church will be young men and men of a very high order." Indeed, it was a common saying that while parents remained in the old church, sons and daughters went to the new one. Among them were many young families, filling the church school with their 125 youngsters. Some 19 teachers were required to handle the influx.

Birthing of a New Church

The Edwards Church as it appeared circa 1860.

With enthusiasm running high, the youthful congregation purchased the lot at the corner of Main and Old South streets (the present Foster and Farrar block). Mr. Todd's diary noted that the land was bought from "a bitter Unitarian; nobody expected he would sell, and yet he has done so." By this time the minister's family had settled in the newly purchased parsonage on Market Street. Fittingly enough—on Independence Day—the 1833 cornerstone was laid. Meanwhile, the town hall and then the Baptist Church hosted the new congregation while they waited for a building of their own.

On Christmas Day the Edwards meetinghouse was dedicated. With no little pride, Mr. Todd wrote that "the building was considered as handsome as anything in New England outside of Boston." Perhaps a more objective eye would make an

Bid Us God Speed

exception of the soaring grandeur of the First Church across the street. But the new building did have a sense of permanency with its sturdy white-painted brick and simple dignity in its Greek Revival style. In a day when volunteer bucket brigades were more dash than splash, any walls of fireproofed material were felt to be a real plus. A basement lecture room was provided with an entrance on Old South Street.

The Main Street doors led to the sanctuary. Straight ahead and rising toward the heavens—or at least to the gallery—was the pulpit. Winding steps flanked both sides as in earlier Congregational churches. Not at all traditional was a "round transparency" directly over the pulpit. Some seventy-five years later Christopher Clarke recalled that on it "was painted the figure of a dove which seemed to me very beautiful, and made a lasting impression upon my youthful mind. It certainly was an original novel departure from the usual church decorations of that period."

Likely the pews were similar to those of the old church —enclosed and rather high with a door to each. Able to seat a congregation of six hundred, they were a very real source of income. Each New Year's Day the pews were rented at public auction. The first auction in 1834 realized between $9,000 and $10,000—a tidy sum for a single afternoon. The minister noted happily: "So we shall have no trouble in paying for the beautiful house."

Briefly, the six pews facing either side of the pulpit went for $11 to $16, with those nearest the preacher costing $11. Perhaps the lofty pulpit gave anyone seated there a crick in the neck, and therefore deserved a lesser price. The center pews at the front cost $17, and for those with heavier wallets or a bit of prestige, the middle sections sold for $36. For anyone of modest means, there were bargains to be had along the walls at $2.

There was seating in the gallery as well. Hard by the door upstairs was a long seat marked "B.M." A like seat with "B.W." flanked the other side of the door. Henry Gere, in his "Remembrances," could not recall a single "colored person" in one of them. These segregated pews were discontinued in 1850, an action long overdue in this antislavery stronghold of Northampton.

In front of these seats a number of places were set aside for the choir. Music has always been an exciting and inspirational experience at Edwards for these last 150 years. Even before their

Birthing of a New Church

Sale of Pews.

On Monday, the 31st inst. at 1 o'clock, P. M., will be sold at Public Auction, within the Edwards Church, upwards of **FORTY PEWS**; the situation of which may be seen, on plans of the house, at the office of Samuel Wells, store of Stoddard & Lathrop, book-store of J. H. Butler, and at the shop of Enos Parsons.

The Pews will be put up at a reduction of 40 per cent. from the original valuation, and sold without reserve. The choice of one or more Pews may be put up at each time.

Such an opportunity for obtaining Pews on the most reasonable terms, may not occur again in this place. The location of the house in which said Pews are situated is good, and the building substantial. It is also known that no member of this Church or Society is taxed, but each pays what he chooses.

Conditions of Sale—1-4th cash; the balance, 1-2 in 8 months, 1-2 in 16 months, with interest from date of sale. The deeds to be delivered to purchasers on paying the last instalment.

Northampton, Dec. 26, 1838.

Broadside advertising sale of pews, 1838.

building was completed, parishioners were enjoying special music. A violin, a new double bass viol, a "common" viol, and flutes accompanied the choristers. In the new church there were many who felt that an organ should be installed. Others were against the idea. The pastor had no wish to take sides and wrote, in 1835, "I believe they will have an organ, but it may be the means of splitting us all to pieces." If one had been acquired (because of a later fire, our records on this point are incomplete), it would have been the first such in Hampshire County.

The most significant addition to the new church, however, was the handsome silver communion set. On each vessel was engraved the inscription: "Presented to the Edwards Church in token of Christian Unity by the First Church in Northampton, Mass. 1834." Encircling this inscription was a vine, under which was written "I am the true vine." Under the branches was "Ye are the branches" and, on the upper side of the vine, "And the blood of Jesus Christ cleanseth us from all sin." This token of brotherly love between parent and offspring was truly a sacrificial gift. The $500 cost was a large part of the $1,200 total then in the First Church's treasury.

As for the Reverend Todd's ministerial philosophy, he made it clear at the outset that this new church would always cherish

Bid Us God Speed

Communion silver presented to the Edwards Church by the First Church, 1834.

"as her heart's blood the doctrines which Jonathan Edwards taught." He was not a fire-and-brimstone preacher, but he did emphasize such classical theological doctrines such as predestination, the Trinity, and Original Sin. Old church members and Jonathan Edwards himself would have felt quite at home at Edwards. When a son was born to the young Todds on December 6, 1833, he was named Jonathan Edwards. Appropriately, the infant was the first to be baptized in Edwards Church.

As has been the case with every minister throughout time, Todd had concerns over those in his flock who felt that Christianity was a sometime thing. "Even in this beautiful valley," he wrote, "where the waters murmur soft as those of Silva, the heart of man is selfish and proud and full of sin. The waters of life flow unheeded and there is more eagerness to see Henry Clay than to see One greater than he." These were hard words, but there were changes in the wind. The spirit of Christian

Birthing of a New Church

outreach and brotherly love was becoming evident in his young and receptive parishioners. Mr. Todd feared that the temperance, antislavery, child labor abuse, and education movements—although worthy—would dilute the Bible's message of the paramount importance of seeking one's own salvation.

But Mr. Todd's strong hand was lost when he accepted a call to a new parish. It was time for the Todds and their growing family of four children—including little Jonathan—to take leave of their now sizable congregation. On October 6, 1836, the pastor wrote, "Tomorrow we set out for Philadelphia amidst the tears of my people and in full grief ourselves." They boarded the yellow stage in front of Warner's Tavern and were off for the challenge of another newly built church. The Todds' stay in Northampton was short, but their influence was lasting.

Until a new minister could be found, the gap was admirably filled by Edwards Church deacons. There was Thomas Napier, a Scot of rare common sense with a deep, abiding faith in the church and a generosity to match it. Enos Clark, a thirty-year member of First Church, brought maturity and wisdom to any problems that arose. Josiah Whitney, a scholar and successful businessman, served as treasurer while James Hibben, the church's first clerk, continued in that role. William Stoddard led the Sabbath school as superintendent. In fact, he would give his energies to that position for the next half century. These and other members held the new church together until a leader was chosen.

1836-1842

John Mitchell

A Growing Congregation

BEFORE THE YEAR ENDED, the Reverend John Mitchell had answered the call, and another yellow stagecoach —this time from Hartford—had delivered a much-anticipated passenger. Mr. Mitchell was something of a change.

Bid Us God Speed

"Bland" is the word that comes to mind; he was rather pale and stooped. Quiet, conservative, and cautious, he would kindle few fires. It was said that he was a better writer than a preacher. Sickly from the start, he was unable to preach his introductory sermon because of hoarseness. But he had a level, cool head and was a man with whom one could sit down and talk out a problem.

There were always problems, as in any rapidly changing society. By 1836 the Northampton-New Haven Canal was doing a brisk business, and the many new factories along Mill River were floating their goods down to coastal buyers at New Haven. Then came the great depression of 1837-39, and businesses everywhere were hard hit. The silk industry was one of many that went under. An occasional mulberry tree may still be found in the area—each a monument to the failure of this business in 1839.

Northampton rebounded quickly. There is no doubt about it: the Protestant ethic of hard work, honest dealings, thrift, and a dash of Yankee ingenuity continued giving the good life to the town. It was seen as evidence of God's approval. Certainly there should be as much concern for others as for one's own salvation and well-being. This was apparent in the growing popularity of reform movements. Meanwhile, the good health that seemed to bypass Mr. Mitchell became the goal of the average citizen here and everywhere. Water cures were notable attractions in Northampton by the early 1840s.

Dr. Sylvester Graham, the "Philosopher of Sawdust Pudding," is remembered by the graham cracker—his contribution to a wholesome diet. He found it healthful to march himself down Main Street and past Edwards Church in his dressing gown for a dip at Lickingwater crossing at the foot of Old South Street. Tolerance for anyone who is different has long been a characteristic of this Connecticut River town.

Social activities centered around the church. Christopher Clarke recalled the Friday prayer meetings in the basement vestry. One could count on Deacon Asahel Abels to raise the rafters with some of the good old hymns. A touch of romance was not wanting. "There were no streetlights in those days," Clarke wrote, "and it was, of course, an imperative duty to see that our favorite maidens had safe escorts, and if we did not arrive in time for the beginning of the service, we were on hand at the vestry door when the meeting ended."

Of interest was a "Donation Party" in 1839 for the Mitchells.

A Growing Congregation

The pastor described the event in some detail in a letter to his mother. Thirty to forty ladies, armed with needles and thread, descended on the parsonage early one Wednesday afternoon and tackled the pile of dry goods and clothing that had been delivered earlier. That evening the men arrived to begin what seemed the most "cheerful" and lively event of the year. Tea was served, and by 9:00 P.M. the table groaned under the weight of "a variety of rich cakes, lemonade, oranges, etc." Other donations of a more lasting nature were two barrels of flour, seventy-five pounds of brown sugar, and a keeping room rug (a treasure at a time when many families could cover their floors only with paint and perhaps stenciled designs). Mrs. Mitchell was remembered handsomely with a fine worktable, an exquisite shawl, three or four new dresses, four pairs of shoes, and so on. The minister and his sons were the better for clothing and sundry gifts, including a purse of $35.

Such was the affection for this mild-mannered minister. But repeated illnesses had taken their toll, and Mr. Mitchell ended the second pastorate at Edwards after some six years.

1843-1846

E. P. Rogers

A Personality in the Pulpit

THE NEW PASTOR, E. P. Rogers of Chicopee Falls, needed no long-distance stagecoach. He also needed nothing in the way of personality! If the pastoral committee was looking for an exact opposite of their kindly but rather lackluster Mr. Mitchell, here was the discovery of the century! The Reverend A. M. Curtin, pastor of the First Church in Easthampton, used such superlatives as "bright-hearted, healthy, hale and well met, handsome in form, face, features. Of easy and graceful manners, ready in speech, had on his lips a pleasant word for every passer by. Knew everybody, men, women, child—knew them by name, and he called them all by their

Bid Us God Speed

names"—and, in comparison to the previous pastor—he "never passed people in the street without noticing them. Was never caught looking on the sidewalk, and wrapped in brown study—never that."

But could he preach? The Reverend Colton, a nonbiased contemporary, wrote:

In one respect Brother Rogers surpassed any preacher I have ever known–viz. in his easy and fluent use of a manuscript–reading as if he didn't read–catching the words by glances so quick as leave you in doubt whether he takes his eyes off you at all. And he has in an admirable degree that quick and off-hand readiness in all his mind and manners. Bright-minded; cup full and running over with the oil of gladness.

In sum, the Reverend Rogers was enough to give any pastor within earshot an inferiority complex. But in all two few years his dynamic personality propelled him to a large and influential Dutch Reformed Church on Fifth Avenue in New York City. Perhaps he sped to his new post on the newly opened railroad line that ran south through Springfield.

1848-1851

George E. Day

Reforms and Christian Ideals

BY THE MID-NINETEENTH century, the many reform movements had laid bare some of the more glaring evils of the day. Slavery continued to stir the nation's conscience. The Underground Railroad had been organized in 1838, and an ever increasing number of southern slaves were hidden in Northampton during their journey to freedom. At this time there were well over five hundred abolition societies in the North. Meanwhile, in 1842, Massachusetts passed an act requiring a minimum education for every child, and no more than a

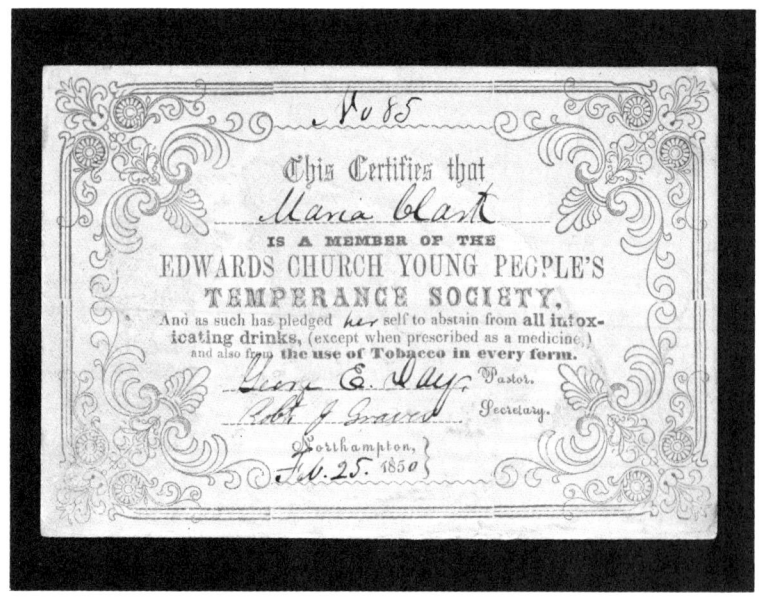

Temperance card, 1850.

ten-hour day in factory labor for children under the age of ten. The first Women's Rights Convention was held in New York some six years later.

There were other concerns. The war with Mexico exploded in 1846. Locally and elsewhere the great influx of Irish famine refugees arrived, desperate for work in the face of our country's seven-year depression. Now, if the Edwards congregation expected a second Jonathan Edwards to rise up from the pulpit and lead a fiery crusade for human rights and justice for all, the Reverend George Day would have been found wanting. Instead, this gentle man reemphasized the importance of living up to one's Christian ideals. After all, if there were consideration and love for one's neighbor, there would be little need for the current reform efforts.

When a company of young men caught the gold-digging fever in 1849 and were ready to leave by the long Isthmus route to California, Mr. Day addressed them at the First Church. He reminded the group that they represented the high moral standards of the town and should work in harmony while observing temperance and chastity. Profanity and gaming were to be

Bid Us God Speed

avoided, and the Sabbath respected. Finally, he impressed the gathering that there was a treasure to be gained in a life to come, "vaster, richer than the mines of Mexico, or the wealth of India." The address was printed in a pamphlet, and fifty copies were supplied to the company—reminders that the hometown churches expected no compromise in their standards.

In his quiet and scholarly way, Mr. Day touched the lives about him with love and affection. Certainly he had not an enemy in the world, and any hard word against this kindly Christian would be unthinkable. His good works were lost to the congregation but not forgotten when he became a professor at Yale Theological Seminary.

1852-1879

Gordon Hall

Building a New Church

EDWARDS CHURCH seemed destined to attract short-term ministers, Yale men all, with an ability for leadership that did not go unnoticed by other pastoral committees. So the search for the fifth pastor began. To the great good fortune of the Edwards Society, Dr. Gordon Hall, also a Yale graduate, accepted the call. He was the son of Gordon Hall, one of the four Williams College theological students who had been caught in a shower back in 1805 and had found shelter in a haystack. When the conversation turned to the need for missionaries in foreign lands, the famed Haystack Conference was born. Inspired, the elder Hall pioneered the founding of the American Board of Foreign Missions before sailing to do missionary work in India. There must have been a few spare moments in his busy life, for in Bombay he met and married an English woman, Margaret Lewis. Of the four children born to this union, two died in infancy. Later, the elder Reverend Hall succumbed to cholera. These tragedies were compounded when Mrs. Hall and her remaining two children sailed for home. One

Building A New Church

of the youngsters died en route and was buried at sea. Young Gordon, the only child left, and his mother finally arrived in Salem to begin a new life. Many years later Margaret Hall accompanied her son, his wife, and their five sons and one daughter to Northampton to help in the running of the family.

With this legacy of Christian dedication, the Reverend Dr. Hall became our man for all seasons. Although early descriptions are sketchy, in the later years of his long pastorate he was said to be very distinguished in appearance—tall, spare and slightly stooped, and with spectacles that framed his "keen and thoughtful eyes." The congregation considered him modest and unassuming, unselfish, prudent, and blessed with uncommon wisdom. In 1879 the *Gazette* stated that "He was a pure man—pure in thought, speech and in action." Indeed, there was a "delicacy and refinement" about the man.

Congregationalism continued to change with the times. The old theological philosophies of personal salvation broadened into concern for one's neighbor. Antislavery, temperance, better general education, woman suffrage, and improved working conditions for children all had their advocates in the United States. Now the thrust became worldwide, as missionaries carried the Word of God to foreign lands. The new minister was a champion of his father's "mission" in life, and Edwards became something of a center for collecting monies and goods for many foreign missions and hospitals. More important, the church sponsored a number of its own people for service in the field—a local version of "Practice what you preach."

This enthusiasm to share their God and Savior with everyone deserves more mention later. To return to Dr. Hall and his influence on his own congregation. His love of children was reflected in a growing Sunday school. In 1833 there had been 125 pupils; in 1845 there were 130; but by 1872 attendance had more than doubled, to 266. It should be noted that two years after the church's founding, a school library was established to stimulate religious reading among the young. By 1845 there were upward of seven hundred volumes. In his home, Dr. Hall brought up his own children with a kind of order and authority that required no stern reprimands on his part.

If this man seems too good to be true, the regard of his parishioners for him shows otherwise. When the Halls arrived in Northampton, the family rented the brick house at 84 Elm Street. The purchase price of $3,000 was well beyond the minis-

Bid Us God Speed

terial salary for these years. Quietly, $1,500 was raised among the congregation in spite of a long-standing depression. An anonymous member matched this amount, and the deed was purchased in Dr. Hall's name. One evening the Halls were startled to find great numbers of their Edwards friends dropping by. It was an emotional moment when the deed for their house was presented to them. Overcome by such an outpouring of love and generosity, the minister said, "you have, by this act, married me to this church as long as I am able to serve it."

But there were dark days ahead for the nation. Abraham Lincoln, when accepting the nomination for United States senator from Illinois, said, "a house divided against itself cannot stand. I believe this government cannot endure permanently half slave and half free." Several years later, when the Confederate states seceded from the Union, Lincoln, now president, mobilized what was left of the nation. The antislavery drive, begun so long ago in the North, had exploded into the Civil War.

Preservation of the Union came at a fearful cost. Locally, Company C returned to Northampton on June 26, 1864, with only 220 men left out of the 1,000 who had marched off three years earlier. Capt. James Weatherall's body came home that same June day to a funeral service at Edwards. The church was filled to overflowing. This outpouring of grief from old friends and comrades in the field left no room for any victory celebration. Some church members felt it was difficult to love one's enemies when the lives of so many of their young men had been sacrificed to the rebels' musket balls.

This was not so for President Lincoln, however, who proclaimed in his second inaugural address: "malice toward none . . . charity for all." Then came the unthinkable. Lincoln was shot to death five days later at Ford's Theater in Washington, D.C. Dr. Hall took to the pulpit with fire in his eyes. In his sermon, "President Lincoln's Death—Its Voice to the People," he stated that the Union had been preserved through the nation's sacrifices and the president's wisdom and leadership.

Unfortunately, Mr. Lincoln had been extending the olive branch of conciliation rather than the rod of punishment. Such a "mistaken and ruinous policy" would make treason trivial, make confiscation of property improper, and give the traitorous Confederate leaders continued control over southern affairs. Blacks would be free in name only—second-class citizens who must depend on their recent owners for their livelihood. The

Building A New Church

After the fire of 1870.

assassin's bullet should shock the nation into taking a sterner approach to the reconstruction of the south. Lincoln's death served as a warning— a "voice to the people," and it was high time the rebel leadership be brought to account.

I say this—the halter for intelligent, influential traitors. But to the honest boy, to the dedicated men, who has been deceived into rebel ranks, I would extend clemency. I would say, return to your allegiance, renew your support to the government and become a good citizen. But the leaders I would hang.

There should be no more turning of the other cheek—enough was enough.

Then came an unexpected calamity to the Edwards Church Society. On May 19, 1870, the adjacent Hunt building caught fire, and soon the church was hopelessly engulfed in flames. Adding kick to punch, the two-year-old organ—the first large organ in town—was also totally destroyed.

Yankees have never let their thrifty natures stand in the way of generosity. And generous the Edwardsites were, in spite of the postwar depression that flattened every pocketbook. A closer cooperation and a deeper dedication seemed to spring from the ashes. By the autumn of 1870 a new and larger church

Bid Us God Speed

was under construction at the corner of Main and State streets.

The face of Main Street was changing rapidly, for trouble seemed to come in bunches. In 1870 the Warner House and Tavern on the north side and the brick-and-wooden Lyman block to the west were completely gutted by fire. Then, six years later, the handsome First Church burned to the ground, owing to the carelessness of a workman who was making repairs. The fire spread to the adjoining Whitney block. For the moment, Northampton was a sorry spectacle. But, as with the building of Edwards, those blackened gaps were shortly replaced by new brick and stone buildings. Downtown Northampton began to take on the appearance that is familiar to us today.

Certainly Dr. Hall had seen his congregation through some trying times. But, after completing a quarter of a century of his pastorate, he was able to say "that no deacon for 25 years had passed out of office, except by removal from town or by decease." The congregation, he went on, had acted harmoniously with an unselfish spirit, aiming for the general good by supporting the will of the majority. In sum, "We have had no strife or divisions."

Well, this was not exactly the case. Deacon William H. Stoddard, reminiscing some years later, did take exception to the latter statement. The one sour note seemed to have involved the organ for the newly built church. "An unwarranted extravagance," said some. Their point was well taken, for debt on the new building would only be increased with the purchase. However, at the personal expense of several modest, unnamed individuals, the organ was installed for a trial period of three years. It was an interesting strategy, for after that time the initial donors felt that the congregation would unite and defray the remaining cost. And so they did.

The beloved Dr. Hall in 1879, after nearly thirty years as pastor, succumbed to typhoid pneumonia. At his funeral, the *Gazette* described the interior of the church as being draped in black, and on the casket was a sheaf of wheat "emblematic of the purity and ripeness" of the deceased. There followed a two-year interval without a pastor as a committee searched, seemingly in vain, for a replacement. Dr. Hall's influence is still felt in the twentieth-century life of Edwards Church, particularly in the mission field.

For example, four years after his death, the Gordon Hall Mission Band was organized in honor of the minister and his

Building A New Church

The second Edwards Church in the early 1900s.

Bid Us God Speed

missionary father. Be not misled. It was made up not of musicians playing on street corners but of a group of ladies dedicated to sending the Christian Word to India, Turkey, and the Pacific islands. In addition, there were the Ladies' Home Missionary Society, the Edwards Church Division of the Northampton Auxiliary of the Women's Board of Missions, the Young Ladies' Mission Circle, and the Young People's Missionary Society.

In 1883 a small religious newspaper, the *Morning Star* (named for the missionary ship serving the Pacific islands), described the extent of the Congregational church's missionary efforts in that part of the world. Eight male and nine female missionaries brought Christ's message to the inhabitants of the thousands of small islands of Micronesia. They had established forty-five churches with over four thousand members!

Also noted was that for every dollar spent on mission work, the United States received ten dollars in return. This was because the underdeveloped countries were in need of manufactured goods in general, and especially of plows, reapers, knitting machines, outline maps, cabinet organs, and the like. The newspaper went on to say:

An old New England wagon maker was persuaded to give ONE DOLLAR *to missions in the Sandwich Islands, grumbling all the while that he might as well* THROW IT AWAY, *but afterward, imagine his astonishment when he received an order for twenty carts of ninety dollars each, from that same country, and in short, no enterprise in this world has ever paid as grandly as that of foreign missions.*

1882-1891

Isaac Clark

Emphasis on Sabbath School Education

AFTER A TWO-YEAR search, the committee in charge invited the Reverend Isaac Clark to join the Edwards family. His installation banquet, served "smoking hot," was something of a Thanksgiving feast after the lean months

Awards of Merit.

without a pastor. There were hot stewed oysters, roasted turkeys, roasted beef, chicken pie, meat and squash pies, puddings, coffee, bread and biscuits, oranges, apples, nuts, raisins, and grapes. Too, in spite of the season, there were flowers everywhere. Mr. Clark must have been pleased with this new brick church. The stained-glass windows were outstanding reminders of those who gave so much of themselves to Edwards. One honored Dr. and Mrs. Gordon Hall. Others, including Sidney E. Bridgman, thirty years a deacon; Henry S. Gere, owner and editor of the *Hampshire Gazette*, and his wife Martha; Benjamin Cook, first mayor of Northampton; and Deacon William Jones, who served from 1876 to 1911; were among those memorialized.

Northampton people have always placed a high priority on education. Added to an excellent public school system, which included Smith's Agricultural School, were the private Gothic Seminary for Girls, the Round Hill School for Boys, the Mills and Howe law school, the Mary Burnham School, Northampton School for Girls, Clarke School for the Deaf, the Hill Institute, the

Bid Us God Speed

first free kindergarten in the country, and Smith College for young women.

From the very beginning Edwards looked to the spiritual growth of the young people in its charge. Yet it was realized that the Sabbath school provided only brief exposure to Christian ideals. Therefore, shortly after the church dedication, young people's prayer meetings were organized. Held each Sunday evening, sometimes at the Hospital Hill Chapel, the services were very popular. The church school itself moved ahead with varied programs and, by 1888, had reached a total enrollment of 439 pupils.

The celebrating of Christ's birthday passed with little notice before 1850. The Victorian era placed increasing emphasis on the spirit of giving—tinged with a bit of paganism in the form of ornamental Christmas trees and Old Saint Nicholas himself. The church notice for December 1891 was characteristic:

The children of the Primary Class are invited to meet in the Chapel at half-past four o'clock Friday afternoon when an entertainment especially for them will be provided. At six o'clock supper will be served to which all members of the Sunday School are cordially invited. Santa Claus will visit the School later in the evening and asks that each child bring some small gift for the tree. These will be collected by him and carried to poorer children.

As times change, succeeding generations of churchgoers have been aware of some of the difficulties of keeping the Sabbath day holy. Our Pilgrim and Puritan forefathers set aside each Sunday for the solemn worship of God. This practice was deeply imbedded in the roots of Edwards Church. For the youngsters it meant fidgeting on hard benches for seemingly endless sermons and afterward being forbidden to release their pent-up energies through play. But there was a solution—"Sunday toys" that would be instructive in the words of the Bible and Christian living in general. There were blocks that could become a church, music box hymns, and card and board games that subtly gave instructions for a virtuous life. Most popular was Noah's Ark and its endless parade of paired creatures. Many a father whittled his impressions of these furred and feathered passengers during the long winter evenings. For those old enough to read, "penny" books were available with biblical stories.

Emphasis on Sabbath School Education

Sunday toys.

Today many of the older members of the congregation may remember that the Sunday "funny papers" were not considered fit Sabbath reading. Playing cards, dancing, and any sort of labor were frowned upon.

To return to the Reverend Clark: church records give little information or insight into the character of the man. A *Gazette* comment on his farewell sermon is intriguing, however: "Some unpleasantness has arisen over the manner in which his resignation was brought about, but through it all Mr. Clark has born himself with dignity, forbearance and kindness." In a letter giving thanks for a farewell gift, the minister wrote, "These testimonies of hearts and tongues are very grateful to us after the shock and sorrow which came upon us—when and how you all know."

Bid Us God Speed

1892-1898

Paul Van Dyke

Something for Everyone

WE CAN ALSO OFFER little on the life and personality of Paul Van Dyke, the seventh pastor of Edwards. As for his congregation, there was something for everyone. Options in 1892 included the Sunday service and church school, at 4:00 P.M. the regular meeting of the Young Men's Christian Association, at 6:00 P.M. the Young People's Society of Christian Endeavor, and at 7:00 P.M. the Evening Worship Service. The Ladies' Prayer Meeting was held on Tuesday, as was the Women's Christian Temperance Union gathering. On Thursday the Mothers' Meeting gave sundry household hints on such subjects as "Cooking For Invalids," "How Shall Children be Wisely Disciplined," "Sympathy With Children," and "How Shall we Make Our Children Helpful?" The Ladies' Home Mission Society met that same day. On Friday evenings was the meeting on "Prayer, Praise and Meditation on the Scriptures"; and, of course, there were the periodic gatherings of the four Mission Circles and the Junior Auxiliary, church committees, music rehearsals, and the like. Until 1898, the men seemed largely bypassed. Then the well-known Men's Club came into being with its monthly meetings, prominent speakers, and large attendance.

If one still had a few idle hours, there was the Young People's Society, which "Voted to educate half an American Indian by raising $35 before June of 1892." Fortunately, the young people of First Church voted to educate his other half. Or one could attend the Christian Endeavor's "Old-fashioned Sewing Bee," a talk on "Temperance," or the "Chrysanthemum Musical in the church parlor. Plants and flowers on sale. Admission 15c." There was also an ongoing collection of papers and magazines for the reading pleasure of the lumbermen in Wisconsin.

Now that the electric streetcars had replaced the old horse-drawn cars, there was little excuse for not getting to all those

meetings on time. In 1896 inventor Charles Duryea drove the first gasoline combustion car from Springfield to Northampton. It was believed to be the start of America's love affair with the horseless carriage.

Duryea's achievement also marked the beginning of the end of the church's heavy schedule of societies, clubs, and meetings in general. Automobiles would one day be more affordable, carrying the family away from social activities that had been centered in the church.

In 1897 the Edwards Society purchased the house at Seven Paradise Road for a parsonage. One year later Mr. Van Dyke resigned to become a faculty member at his alma mater. He was a popular minister, and his parting was regretted.

1899-1902

Peter McMillan

"The Trenda" Success

HE REVEREND Peter McMillan made his brief appearance on the Edwards scene, then was dismissed. A short account in the *Gazette* reported,

Rev. Mr. McMillan says that statements made in the morning papers are misleading. He has a business proposition under consideration which assures him double the salary he is now receiving. He had experience with Western railroads and lands before entering the ministry and is not unprepared for business life but he states that he prefers and intends to remain in the ministry under certain conditions.

Obviously, these conditions were unacceptable to the congregation.

Apparently, Mr. McMillan's departure put no damper on the social triumph of the decade. The *Gazette* in 1902 enthusiasti-

Bid Us God Speed

cally pronounced that "The Trenda" supper given by the ladies of Edwards Church on the previous evening was distinctly a social and financial success. Guests were given coupon tickets with "stop-over privileges for three highly decorated homes." Miss Maltby's home on Elm Street was transformed into a colonial mansion of Old Virginia. Twenty-five handsomely costumed girls from Smith College ushered the guests to tables. "Colored" waiters served creamed oysters, croquettes, corn pudding, coffee, and rolls. A quartet of "colored" young men furnished the background music.

Then the party-goers traveled on to Japan, conveniently transferred to the nearby home of Miss Bodman. Banners; umbrellas; lanterns; and a college girl, who "executed a most astonishing Japanese bow" but whose Oriental "vocabulary was not very extended," met the ticketholders. Japanese curios were everywhere and were explained by costumed young ladies. In the dining room were varieties of Japanese salads of pickled fish, peppers, and nuts, along with souvenier chopsticks. Fifteen young ladies sang sundry songs, including the Japanese national hymn.

There was no doubt that Mexico had invaded the S. E. Bridgman home. The hallway was festooned with colorful flags, palms, rubber plants, and Mexican curios. Dressed in south-of-the-border clothing, Mr. E. O. Gere carried a large basket of oranges on his head! The guests were ushered into the restaurant, where Spanish ladies "with lace fichus and mantillas, bare arms and much jewelry" assisted men dressed in white duck trousers, Navajo blankets, and sombreros that gave a "kaleidoscope effect." Not to be forgotten were members of the Smith College Mandolin and Guitar Club, strumming away on little balconies and stairways. At any rate, the Edwards music fund was $150 richer when the benefit festivities were over.

"The Trenda" Success

1903-1912

Willis H. Butler

75th Birthday Celebration

THE SEARCH FOR A minister continued with nary a prospect in sight. At the fourth annual meeting of the Men's Club, the Reverend F. L. Goodspeed of Springfield opened his talk by saying that he was the only man left who had not been suggested as a suitable pastor for Edwards Church! The following speaker, the noted author George W. Cable, pointed out that

The religion of today should not leave any time for the discussion of theology. Instead, it should fill the heads of men with so much good that they should be filled with good will for everyone. It should be a religion more closely connected with science and culture than theories.

Mr. Todd, the first minister, would have thrashed in his grave at such thoughts.

One hundred and fifty men were present, for the club was in its upsurge of popularity. It should be noted that many such clubs throughout the country, totaling well over five thousand men, had patterned their meetings after the successful Edwards format.

Finally, the long pastoral search paid dividends. The Reverend Willis H. Butler, then at the First Church of Williamstown, Massachusetts, answered Edwards' call. He was well known for his powerful sermons, and indeed had been selected by Woodrow Wilson as a regular university preacher while still a student at Princeton. In the Edwards Church archives is a book of Mr. Butler's favorite sermons, *The Reality of Things Unseen*, published in 1933. Its introduction emphasized that,

Dr. Butler put all his strength into preparation for his pulpit work. No part of it was slipshod or casual, in substance or in manner. His sermons were in the main addressed to a world in doubt and sorrow, struggling with the mysteries and difficulties of life.

Bid Us God Speed

These were sermons not to be missed by the congregation. In addition, as one member put it, "He knew when to stop."

The year 1908 was well worth remembering. The *Gazette* stated that "No church ever celebrated its 75th birthday under more auspicious circumstances, prosperous, harmonious in all its activities, than does the Edwards Church." Among the speakers was Dr. Isaac Clark of Washington, D.C., who was the minister at the fiftieth anniversary celebration. President L. Clarke Seelye of Smith, also present for that anniversary, brought greetings from the college to the church. He had close ties with Edwards, and he "thanked the church for the great interest that the church had taken in the students of the college, and the spiritual home the church had made for them while they were living for a time away from their home." (This church-college relationship would be an important consideration when the subject of possible sites for the future third building was debated.) Among many others on the program was Christopher Clarke, the venerable old gentleman who recalled many events of the church's founding some seventy-five years before!

The evening program was presented by Professor Story of the Smith College music department. The church quartet, assisted by a chorus of former choir members, illustrated the development of American church music.

1913-1918

Irving Maurer

Impact of Reforms

THE PULPIT SUPPLY committee, having visited the Reverend Washington Irving Maurer in Plymouth, New York, wrote in its report that the members were pleased with his preaching and were "charmed" with his personality. Maurer, they said, was also a crusader for "moral uplift," having been instrumental in closing "the disorderly houses" in

Plymouth. Not only that, but Smith President Marion Leroy Burton, a member of the committee, had known the candidate when Maurer was a student at Yale Theological Seminary. He remembered that the prospective minister "was a fine specimen of a man, physically and intellectually, and best of all was the fact that he had perfect digestion." There would be no need for concern at Edwards Church dinners!

Social reforms with concern for the underprivileged had reached a fever pitch. The new minister and his congregation saw eye to eye on these issues. The previous year, Massachusetts had adopted a minimum wage for women and children—the first in the country. The suffragettes were marching on Washington for the right to vote.

Back in Northampton, a random selection of notes from the Edwards *Weekly Calendar* reflect some of the local interests of those days.

June 6, 1915 Strangers who find it difficult to hear the church service, and who would like to use the Mears telephone, can find out from the ushers which receivers are not in use. Those persons who wish to own their own receiver can arrange to connect their pew by speaking to Mr. Victor N. Lucia of the directors.

June 27, 1915 Thursday 2:30-5:30. The War Relief Association will work in the Chapel. The work we are doing is actually saving lives. Could you come in for an hour and help?
A young Pole of brilliant qualities, fitting himself for work among his countrymen in the Connecticut Valley, will need help to go through medical college. The minister will be glad to receive money or opportunity for work for the young man.

September 12, 1915 At 2:30 and 7:30 on Saturday and Sunday, Sept. 18 and 19, the Flying Squadron of New England will hold meetings in Edwards Church to discuss National Prohibition.

October 10, 1915 The Hampshire County Chapter of the American Red Cross will hold a Mass Meeting in the Academy of Music at 7:45 Sunday evening, October 17th. Mr. Cranston Brenton, New York director of War Relief, will speak.

October 17, 1915 Our Home Missionary Society is asking for Ford

Bid Us God Speed

cars for home missionaries. The first one to be given came from a New England woman. It will be used by a missionary in a mountain region west of the Rockies.

October 31, 1915   The ladies of Edwards Church are to entertain two hundred delegates who will attend the State W.C.T.U. Convention in this city, Nov. 2, Tuesday at dinner and supper.

December 19, 1915   Children, before next Friday leave a little amount of money at the Red Cross headquarters on Center Street, for the relief of children in Belgium and Poland.

January 9, 1916   A boy of seven in Edwards Church Sunday School is greatly in need of an overcoat.

January 20, 1916   Write to our Massachusetts Senators at Washington urging the passage of the Keating-Owen bill prohibiting the inter-state commerce in articles manufactured by children under 14, or by children under 16 working more than 8 hours per day.

March 5, 1916   The minister and the boys of the Pastor's class will tramp. Bring ten cents and bacon.

April 30, 1916   Tomorrow morning the saloon comes back to Northampton after a year under the ban. . . . Inasmuch as the saloon keeper is again a legally accepted member of our community, we wish to give him a list of rules where by his business may be as respectable as possible.

1. Never cash a pay check.
2. Never permit treating.
3. Never sell adulterated liquors.
4. Send out all college boys.
5. Keep a card index of your customers. It will help you to keep track of the funerals. It will also give you information regarding the number of children, and will establish the limit of the man's financial ability.

May 7, 1916   A supper in the church parlors will be served by the Aloha Guild for 35 cents. Strawberry shortcake, 10 cents extra.

May 14, 1916   The Christian Endeavorers will have a Box and

Impact of Reforms

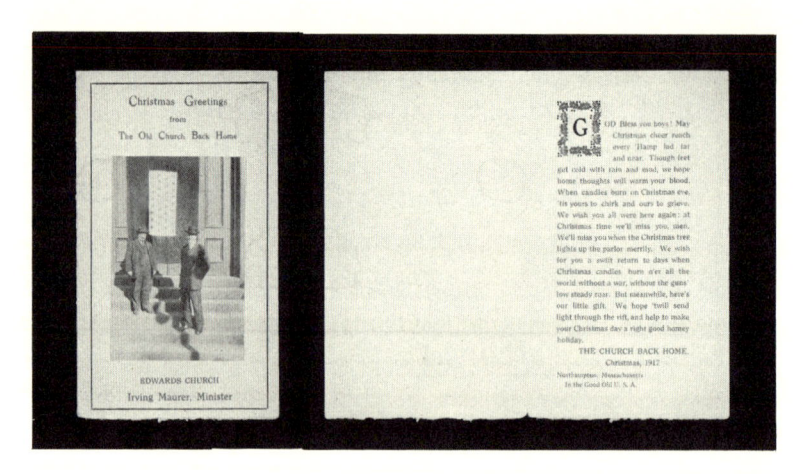

Christmas greetings from back home, 1917.

Rubber Social, Tuesday evening, May 16. Come and bring your old rubbers. Girls bring lunch for two.

July 2, 1916   The efforts to hold a community Independence Day celebration are worthy of the support of all our people. Let all turn out for the Sports and for the illumination. It is something that the city can do together.

January 7, 1917   Friday 2:00 A Sewing Meeting in the Guild Room. Work will be begun for sending a barrel to Piedmont College. Second-hand clothing of all kinds is asked for.

March 25, 1917   Do not miss the pageant given in this church Tuesday, March 27. All the churches co-operating in the Mission Study Class will be represented in the different episodes: over one hundred persons are taking parts and it will be an impressive showing of what our Home Missionary Societies are doing.

Church calendars took on less importance in the days following the United States' declaration of war against Germany. On June 17, 1917, Mr. Maurer offered a "War Commencement" prayer. He concluded:

Now when the life before us is swirling and eddied by the sinister cross purposes of a world at war, grant to us on the one hand

Bid Us God Speed

undiminished loyalty to our vision and on the other hand strength of will and a great love to endure the sorrows and the death for the sake of truth by which alone the world can build anew. Give us a part to play in the defeat of human oppression, and sustain us, in the doing of our work, with the spirit that was in Jesus.

There were sorrows and deaths aplenty to come on the battlefields of Europe. Three young men from Edwards lost their lives in the conflict: Clifford Ballard, Donald Clark, and Henry Wood.

One of the bright spots in these bleak war years was the 1918 Community Sing and Christmas Pageant. It was sponsored by the Protestant churches of the city and held at the Academy of Music, and the crowd was so large that hundreds had to be turned away. They were denied the pleasure of seeing the angel "in shimmering white with flaming wings," as reported by the *Gazette*. Concerning the Shepherds, "Their attitude of awe and wonder was well done, and their voices natural rather than theatrical." The *Gazette* went on to say that "the keynote was religious simplicity rather than dramatic effect, and it was extremely effective." Santa Claus was among the missing.

1919-1928

Kenneth B. Welles

Pride in President Coolidge

THE REVEREND Kenneth B. Wells became the new pastor of Edwards Church just in time to settle into the new parsonage at 27 Crescent Street. He was also in time to see the years of temperance work succeed with the passage of the Eighteenth Amendment. An old advertising catch phrase became "See America Thirst." Under the dynamic leadership of Susan B. Anthony, women's right to vote finally became law in 1920.

These were lawless times as well. Rum-running activities during Prohibition ushered in the gangster era. Hard times or

Calvin and Grace Coolidge in front of their Massasoit Street home.

otherwise, Edwards Church was growing and prospering. In 1921 the Welle-Kum-In Club was formed and, in spite of its name, had a fine turnout of young people. For the first time, an assistant minister was hired—and necessarily so, for church membership had grown to 972 by 1924. Mr. Wells emphasized, however, that this figure was not because of male members. Out of an average Sunday attendance of 480, only 116 were men, and their numbers were decreasing steadily.

One man was definitely not in his pew that year. Calvin Coolidge was elected president, and the nation's capital was hardly a Sunday drive away. Mr Wells, with no little pride, told the congregation that "We are the President's own church. We should give him some of the spiritual help he needs." A letter of support was sent, and from the White House came a thank-you letter to Coolidge's fellow Congregationalists. His term of office was marked by prosperity and personal popularity. With down-to-earth Yankee wisdom and frugality, he championed ideas and ideals that were appreciated by the average American.

Three years later, President Coolidge, always the master when it came to economy of money or words, announced, "I do not choose to run for President in 1928." Speaking of economy, one of the young members of the church had written to Governor Coolidge for a donation back in 1920. His secretary had replied with the following letter: "Governor Coolidge is very glad to contribute towards the C. E. Can Contest and takes pleasure in enclosing herewith a dollar."

1928-1931

James N. Armstrong

Continued Growth

THE REVEREND James Armstrong was summoned from his stay in Rome to become the twelfth minister. Before his arrival, he asked for an updating of the church rolls so that he could call on each member. Indeed, Mr. Armstrong made a remarkable 1,365 calls that first year, no doubt helping to boost the membership to 1,100. Perhaps he added his thoughts to those of Mr. Wells when he learned that 703 were women—outnumbering the men as usual.

The year 1928 was the one in which a union with First Church became a possibility. After several years of intensive study, the Congregational Church School of Northampton was begun. The joint effort brought 334 people together—227 from Edwards (not including the Lyman Bible Student Class) and 107 from the First Church. Classes were divided between the two buildings, and the experiment was entirely successful. Space and equipment could be used to better advantage; the combined teaching staff coordinated efforts for a better religious education; and the large number of schoolmates added to the overall interest of the young people. Cooperation had become a sign of the times. On a larger front, an example had been set by such organizations as the World Court; the Pan American Union; and, in the world of religion, the Federal Council of Churches.

By the end of the first year, membership in the combined

Church School had risen to 364. The children attended worship services in their own church until after the children's sermon, then departed for their classes. Each child's offering was used to support his or her own church and its missionary projects.

Then, out of nowhere, came the stock market collapse in October 1929. The Great Depression crushed the American spirit temporarily. There was little news to be found of church activities. The Reverend Armstrong ended his brief stay in 1932—perhaps exhausted by all those house calls.

1932-1939

Albert J. Penner

Our 100th Anniversary

DEPRESSION OF A different sort permeated the nation—and Northampton in particular when Calvin Coolidge died suddenly at his home, The Beeches, on January 5, 1933. Two days later the eyes of the world were on Edwards Church and the gray-bronze flower-banked coffin that rested in the sanctuary. Perhaps the thrifty and practical "Cal" would have preferred a simple pine box and a lot less fuss. But such was not the lot for a United States president. Old friends and neighbors were given a special hour to enter the black-draped front entrance of the chapel to pass by the president and pay their last respects.

Although the crowds that choked Main Street were unable to attend the short half-hour service (Mr. Coolidge would have favored such brevity), they saw most of official Washington pass through their midst. The pressure of the onlookers was so great that President and Mrs. Hoover had more than a little difficulty reaching the church. Among the notables were Mrs. Franklin D. Roosevelt and son James, Chief Justice Charles Evans Hughes, Secretary of State Henry L. Stimson, Justice Harlan Fiske Stone, Secretary of the Navy Charles F. Adams, Governor Joseph B. Ely, and a host of local dignitaries. Grace Coolidge and her son John

Bid Us God Speed

were led to a front pew. The old Coolidge family pew was decked with ribbons and roses and unoccupied.

The church quartet sang "Lead Kindly Light" and "O Love That Wilt Not Let Me Go." Possibly the selections were made by Mrs. Coolidge, long a member of the church music committee. The Reverend Albert J. Penner, acting pastor for the past half year, emphasized in his prayer "the frailty . . . of our life here on earth." He went on to say that the nation, though grief-stricken, was a "thankful nation as well, thankful for the life of him whose death we now mourn."

With the passing of Calvin Coolidge into history, Edwards Church in 1933 looked to its own past as it observed its one hundredth anniversary. Certainly a highlight of the event was the play *The Early Days of Edwards Church*. "Jonathan Edwards" again gave one of his thunderous messages from the pulpit. The Donation Party given to Rev. Mitchell was also reenacted. During anniversary week, Albert J. Penner was formally installed as the thirteenth pastor. He came from the Stockbridge Congregational Church, the town that welcomed Jonathan Edwards after his dismissal from Northampton. Mr. Penner was destined later to become president of the 585 churches in the Massachusetts Congregational Christian Conference.

Also recognized at this time was the history of various church organizations. The Aloha Guild began its many years of service in 1880 as the Young Ladies' Mission Circle. Nine years later the group became the Aloha Mission Circle for "study, sewing and socialbility." In 1902 the name was changed to the Aloha Guild. Many were the gifts and scholarships given through the years, as well as mission assistance and help for the Red Cross and the Society for the Prevention of Cruelty to Children. The Edwards Service Circle, begun in 1924, gave its middle name real meaning. The Mothers' Club, formed in 1925, combined sociability with talks on home and family subjects. Between the years 1876 and 1931, the Women's Union packed off a mountain of clothing to southern schools, Puerto Rico, and our western missions. As for the men—who still seemed to leave much wanting in their Sunday attendance—they rallied to start the 1898 Men's Club, as previously mentioned. The first of its kind in New England, it had grown to well over two hundred members. Meanwhile, their sons had joined the Scouting movement at the church-sponsored Troop 3 from 1918 to 1921. After 1923 it became Troop 101. The Brownies and Girl Scouts later became a part of the

Our 100th Anniversary

The Rev. Dr. Albert J. Penner.

Edwards family. The centennial year promised a busy and fruitful future.

The mission movement continued to grow in service and influence. The following people served Edwards Church in the field:

HOME

Sarah A. Mather, *Hampton, Virginia, and St. Augustine, Florida, 1836-1893.*

Clara Rindge Bingham, *Talladoga, Alabama, 1880-1889.*

Clara E. Ellis, *Tongaloo, Mississippi, 1902-1903.*

Mrs. Edna Wood Turner, *Hindman, Kentucky, 1918-1919; China, 1923-.*

Florence B. Wright, *Tongaloo, Mississippi, Athens, Ala., Memphis, Tennessee, 1920-1923.*

FOREIGN

Sophia Hazen Stoddard, *Persia, 1851-1858.*

Minerva Brewster Bingham, *Gilbert Islands (Micronesia), 1856-1875.*

Ellen C. Parsons, *Turkey, 1875-1880.*

Katherine Hastings Wood, *Ceylon, 1882-1891.*

Bid Us God Speed

Irving F. Wood, *Ceylon, 1885-1889.*

Mary B. Daniels, *Japan, 1889-1909.*

Gertrude Harris, *India, 1910-.*

S. Ralph Harlow, *Turkey, 1912-1916, 1919-1922.*

Marion Stafford Harlow, *Greece, 1930-1931.*

Ethel Tomlinson, *Hawaii, 1915-1917.*

Lora Genevieve Dyer, M.D., *China, 1916.*

Margaret A. Dieter, *China, 1918-1923.*

When the Great Flood of 1936 swamped the town, Edwards Church assisted in the effort to cook and care for the 500 people it left homeless in Northampton. Farther afield, assistance was sent to 150 ministers and their impoverished churches in the drought-stricken Midwest. The hurricane of 1938 did $700 damage to the church—no small sum in those depression years.

Yet, the 1930s had their bright spots. Edwards Church music underwent a renaissance in 1938 with the coming of Verdi L. Reusser. A graduate of Hartford Theological Seminary in Connecticut and the Westminster Choir College in Princeton, New Jersey, Mr. Reusser was well qualified to be the new director of music. In 1882 music was provided by a choir with an occasional quartet supplement. After 1904 a paid quartet was used, with only a rare volunteer choir appearance. Mr. Reusser changed all that with not one but four choirs! Music became a real inspiration for the Sunday service.

The adult choir sang on Sundays, and the initial membership of twenty-six increased to thirty-five before the year's end. Each member gave an average of three hours each week. The Choral Union met alternate Tuesdays with several purposes in mind. It was designed for those who enjoyed singing but were unable to attend the regular choir rehearsals. It also offered members a chance to develop better technique before joining the regular choir. The fifteen-member high school choir provided a proving ground for the adult choir. The Junior Choir of some twenty-seven pupils in the fourth to eighth grades sounded off in occasional church services as well as in the church school.

This impetus of good music brought forth an unusual creation the following year. Called the "Singable Supper," it was hosted by eight members of the choir who brought on the victuals garbed in white caps and aprons. The rest of the choir sang parodies on popular and old songs that described each item on the menu. One hundred and twenty diners managed to avoid indigestion, and at 35 cents a head, it was all one big success.

In the year 1939 everyone was talking about the World's Fair in New York. The choir was especially excited that spring. It was to be part of the National Westminster Choir that was to give a concert at the World's Fair Music Hall. But first, the members spent a week in Princeton rehearsing and socializing. Then for the never-to-be forgotten event, they traveled to New York to take part in the American Church Music Concert held in the shadow of the well-known symbols of the Fair—the trylon and perisphere.

That same year, the first spring concert was performed by the Adult and Junior choirs with the public invited. Christmastime brought a joyous community carol sing. As the church calendar said, it was "Not an Hour of Listening, but one of participation for all." The "all" included Baptist, Methodist, First, and Edwards members who joined in the Christmas song choruses. That enthusiastic spark plug, Verdi Reusser, had given music a real vitality during his four-year stay.

Then came more trouble. Nazi Germany was brewing more than enough misery for the world. The rumblings of World War II were evident as early as 1936, and the "Peace Plebiscite," a group formed within the church, planned to do something about it. Eighty-five Edwards people held the position that, as Christians, it would be impossible for them to support or to participate in any war which Congress might declare. By 1937 the church calendar announced:

Your Social Action Committee wishes to suggest that one of your duties as workers for world peace is to bring pressure to bear against the Hill-Sheppard bill now being considered by the House Military Affairs Committee. It is being sold to the country as a measure to take the profits out of war and is thereby fooling many peace lovers into thinking it is a peace measure.

Another notice urged the support of an amendment "to abolish the compulsory feature of military training in schools and colleges." And a later one said: "write a letter to the President, Senators, and Representatives in Congress stating your

Bid Us God Speed

convictions of the vast increases in armament. The threat and use of force has always been disastrous to civilization." However, peace efforts in the church became obsolete with the attack on Pearl Harbor on December 7, 1941.

1939-1945

Paul T. McClurkin

World War II Problems

THE REVEREND Paul T. McClurken carried on the pastorate in very trying times indeed. When war was declared, he told the congregation that "business as usual for the church is past." The pastors of the Protestant churches were

united to work out a common Christian strategy. We must now begin to think of stirring up a united Protestantism to preserve in the world the one message for the world to come, we may defeat our enemies with guns, but we cannot build a new society of justice and brotherhood apart from the Christian program.

For the next decade, the word "unity" appeared frequently in the new *Spire*. (Beginning in 1942, this church newspaper was mailed to the homes of Edwards's 1,120-member congregation for 50 cents a year.) But where unity of purpose in such chaotic times was vital, the actual union of Edwards and the mother church had not yet gained acceptance. In 1942 Edwards voted to operate its own church school separately from the mother church after fourteen years of close cooperation. At the same time, a joint committee from the two churches looking into the possibility of union decided against such a move.

However, the need to conserve fuel for the war effort brought five Protestant churches together to consider joint worship services. On a cold and blustery December evening in 1942, church representatives seemed unable to solve the problem. Ray Gibbons, pastor of the First Church, later wrote about the meeting that

one droll New Englander arose and remarked "My wife usually tells me when I get home that I should have kept still but I think it might help if I repeated a remark I heard when I came to this meeting, 'What this town needs is leadership from the two largest churches, but neither fuel conservation, nor patriotism nor Christianity would get those two Congregational churches together.' " The effect was electric. The ministers of the two named churches immediately withdrew to formulate a definite plan.

The result was that services for the five churches during the winter were divided between Edwards and First for the duration of the war.

Mr. Gibbons continued by saying that

union might be nearer than you think . . . but one wonders whether Christian people can worship together in inspiring service, share their life under a common roof, and not become more convinced of their essential unity. Union may not evolve, but it certainly should be hastened by this experience.

The "University of Life" was one of the many examples of excellent interchurch cooperation. This six-week series of Lenten courses brought 350 people together to "build tomorrow's world." A bonus was the music provided by the choirs from Smith College, Burnham School, the Midshipmen's School, and the Northampton School for Girls, plus a string quartet and the United Choir.

America and its allies were rapidly moving toward victory over the Axis powers. More than an eighth of the Edwards congregation was scattered throughout the world for the war effort. A 1945 vote by Edwards to consider again a merger between the two Congregational churches did not pass. It was felt that no action should be taken at the time because so many young men and women members were away in the armed services.

The churches back home had not forgotten their servicemen. In 1943 a million packages of the unforgettable—not exactly

Bid Us God Speed

gourmet-inspired—K-rations were wrapped with leaflets entitled "Hymns From Home." Some of the favorites were "God Will Take Care of You," "Faith of Our Fathers," "Abide with Me," "There's a Church in the Valley," and "Battle Hymn of the Republic." More popular than K-rations were the boxes of home-baked goodies sent to servicemen by Edwards members. Letters of thanks were sent from distant posts.

George Gay wrote, "you really don't know how much we appreciate it and when I say we I mean the boys in the barracks because regardless of who gets the box we all share and share alike and believe me if you want to see a disappearing act you should see all the foodstuffs go." One year the Reverend McClurken mailed more than ninety handwritten letters to the men and women from Edwards Church. Also sent were six mimeographed sermons. In writing to Dr. McClurken, Pfc. John Lord penned a thoughtful letter which was printed in the January 21, 1945, *Spire*. In part it reads:

Denominational differences lose themselves among soldiers—a mutual understanding replaces them—is this not a worthwhile basis for cooperation among the various Protestant sects after the war? Could this lead to a better understanding and greater tolerance of all religious groups—Catholic, Protestant and Jewish? Many of us feel that that challenge must be met in order that Christianity be enabled to do her share in reconstruction.

Are these thoughts idealistic dreams of men up here—dreams that cannot be fulfilled—or do they constitute a challenge—a challenge to the people at home—and to themselves as well?

In the same 1945 issue of the *Spire*, the Reverend McClurkin stated:

The letters which come to us from our young men indicate that freedom of worship is one of their chief reasons for fighting. It is because of their sacrifice that no one will whisk you off to a concentration camp when you attend a meeting of Edwards Church. Sometimes, however, freedom becomes a cloak for indolence and neglect. Great institutions can die from neglect as well as opposition. If the Christian church does not have your thought, your vision, your presence when it grapples with its place in the tragic world of today, then there is a serious gap in its forces.

World War II Problems

Tolerance, unity, and a deeper commitment to Christian ideals would gain momentum in the postwar years.

1945-1954

L. Byron Whipple

Sprucing up the Old Church

IN 1945 REVEREND Dr. McClurken quietly moved across the Connecticut River to become pastor of the First Congregational Church of Hadley. Five years later, *Gazette* headlines were screaming "Hadley Cleric Resigns, Sees False God in Christ." (Edwards church records give no hint of his harboring any such notions.) His Sunday "sermon" before one hundred dumbfounded churchgoers, as reported in the newspaper, opened with these words: "So much of the present is unsound and untrue that I find myself to have diverged more and more from the traditional orthodox concepts of the church." He stated that he had come to Hadley with but one goal—to find "more of the truth about ourselves."

In his search for "truth," Dr. McClurken claimed that Christianity represented a false god and a false Christ "but more tragically than that, conceals the true God and the true Christ from men." He also felt that there was "more and more evidence that this is not the first and only life you have spent on this earth." Further, the church laws impose a conscience on the world. "Mature people make up their own minds in regard to such things as alcohol, tobacco, gambling and vocabulary—and sexual expression." Then came one more blockbuster: "unfortunately, the church has been so afraid of the sexual component in the expression of love, that it has tended to make love a spiritualzed non-entity, a spurious caricature of the real thing."

He concluded his talk by saying, "I therefore submit my resignation from the church and relinquish my rights as an ordained minister at the close of this service." Before he could leave to head a new "Life Research Institute" in Greenwich,

Bid Us God Speed

Connecticut, the Hampshire Association of Churches concurred with the resignation and, in true Christian spirit, wished him well on his quest for "truth."

To return to Northampton and the 1945 installation of the Reverend L. Byron Whipple. Looking much like a kindly football player, his strong and forthright sermons gave leadership to the confusion of the postwar era. In his first annual report he stated that

The Christian spirit must underlie the basis of a better world. Our armies have defeated the Nazis, but only the Christian spirit can defeat the Nazi spirit. Our armies have beaten down the Japanese, but only the spirit of Christ can conquer the Japanese spirit of militarism. May we ever maintain our world concern, carrying Christ's gospel to every creature.

This missionary spirit, long identified with Edwards, was ongoing. There were sacrificial gifts for the relief of war victims and hungry children in war-ravaged lands. Yearly pledges—by 1947 pew rentals were considered archaic and no longer served as a source of revenue—and "One Great Hour of Sharing" contributions provided food, dollars, and other essentials to the needy of the world.

In 1947 came the invasion of South Korea. By 1951 the nation's anxieties about Asian problems was mirrored in the pastor's New Year's message:

The fact that the President of our United States has declared a state of emergency and is hastening to rebuild the military and industrial strength of our nation, makes it all too clear to us the tragic immenence of a third global war. The Civilian Defense authorities of Northampton have already surveyed the churches of this community, your church among them, for shelter in case of a potential war disaster in this area.

Mr. Whipple called on members of the congregation to rebuild their spiritual strength to meet the current evils.

Global troubles aside, music at Edwards continued to be an inspiration for the congregation. In 1946 a new organ was installed, replacing the old tubular pneumatic instrument with its occasional unexpected wheeze. The old organ, presented to the church in 1897 in memory of Luther and Philena Bodman, had

Sprucing up the Old Church

The Whipple family Christmas card.

been rebuilt in 1924 and added to in 1927. Parts of the old organ were reused in the new one, particularly the old wooden pipes.

However, it takes more than a fine organ to make fine music. It requires an organist and a music director of unusual capabilities. In 1948, to everyone's good fortune, along came Doric Alviani. Perhaps we should say "professor" of music, for that he was at the University of Massachusetts. With an enthusiasm that rivaled that of his predecessor, Verdi Reusser, Alviani reorganized the choirs. Two years later the first WHMP broadcast from Edwards Church brought the Sunday morning service—and the music from the new organ and choir—into area homes.

Meanwhile, Mr. Whipple, who had an abiding interest in children, worked with the young people, including his own. On warm summer nights his neighbors could hear him telling Bible stories to his children on the back porch. In 1947 he reorganized and led Boy Scout Troop 101. That same year, five lucky boys from the Young People's Fellowship accompanied Mr. Whipple on an eight-thousand mile trip! George Ray, Richard Wright, Robert Anderson, Raymond Olson, and Mikkel Kroll were off to Niagara Falls, then Iowa (where the minister preached in his former church), the Black Hills, Yellowstone Park, the Grand Canyon, Pike's Peak, Arizona, New Mexico, and Washington, D.C.

Bid Us God Speed

In 1949 the Young People's Forum maintained a whirlwind schedule. The group made a study of Mormonism; assisted at church suppers and at the church booth at the Three-County Fair and the church fair; raised money with several roller-skating parties, a dance, and a baked bean supper, and it sponsored a splash party at the Y, a scavenger hunt, a hayride, and "several other parties." The spring retreat was a bicycle hike to the Northfield Young Hostel, while the fall retreat was held at the "Den" in Middlefield.

The church school, by 1949, reached an enrollment of 151 youngsters—the largest attendance in six years. By 1954 membership of the Young People's Fellowship had increased by 100 percent. Its annual report to the church noted that "Our advisors have done an excellent job and have been very popular. Perhaps too much so. Two of them, Shirley Damon and Virginia Parsons, have gotten married." Somehow the group found time that year to climb Mount Monadnock, take a trip to Boston to see the Ice Follies, and host a youth group from Danvers.

An aging church building was wearing out with these many active programs. Shortly after Mr. Whipple's arrival the church parlors and offices were remodeled. A new circulating system provided heat in the winter and cool comfort in the summer. It also provided a bill of over $18,000. In addition, there were many more such projects that were crying for help. This was a time for raising solid cash, with any ingenuity that could be mustered.

Beginning in 1946 Edwards Church hosted a real home-cooked food restaurant at the Three-County Fair. This yearly event required the energies of many faithful members, but its reputation grew to such a degree that a permanent restaurant building was provided in 1949.

There were other fundraising efforts such as "Yankee Auctioneer" George Bean's series of auctions at Smith School. The "Birthday Calendar Project" succeeded not only financially but also in extending friendships between members. The annual church fairs, with their novel themes, were a real source of revenue. In the November 1947 *Spire* was the following notice: "Mrs. Earle Parsons, Tel. 2059, will take orders now for mincemeat for your Thanksgiving pies. There will also be mincemeat for sale at the fair."

The Young People's Fellowship served an OLD FASHIONED BAKED BEAN SUPPER the following year. For 75 cents, there was as abundance of baked beans (of course), frankfurts, brown bread, apple

Sprucing up the Old Church

pie, cheese, and coffee—enough for any Saturday supper appetite. The Edwards Church memorial plates went on sale that year at two dollars each sponsored by the Mothers' Club.

One of the most successful fundraising ventures proved to be the Edwards Shop. Sparked by Cora DeRose, volunteers set up shop on Armory Street—just across from the old *Gazette* building. Articles of good, clean but used clothing were brought in by donors, who could put their own prices on the articles if they wished. When sold, two thirds of the selling price went to the donors; the remainder was kept by the shop for the benefit of the church. Any unsold items were marked down one third after eight weeks. If still unsold after sixteen weeks, they were returned to the donors or given to a charity. It was an everybody-wins project, which is still going strong after moving to different sites on Pleasant Street. One final money-making project as listed in the 1954 *Spire* may be mentioned.

To the Women of Edwards Church: Do you bake? If so, do you use Gold Medal flour? If so you will find a coupon on top of the list of recipes which is worth 2½ cents or more, depending on the size of the bag of flour. The Mothers' Club is saving these coupons. We would appreciate anyone saving these and turning them into the Mothers' Club.

What of the men while the women and children labored to refurbish the old church building? The March 1953 *Spire* provided one answer:

Attention Men—Save Monday and Tuesday nights, March 16 and 17 for a cleaning bee. The Board of Directors, upon request from the members of the church [the women?], invite the men of the church to come in their old clothes to wash the walls and woodwork of the parish hall and office. Materials, equipment and refreshments will be provided.

Cosmetic treatment, however, could not take the place of needed major repairs and remodeling, with costs estimated to be from $185,500 to $244,000. Raising funds of such amounts would require all members to double their pledges for at least five years.

One alternative, for many reasons other than cost, was the reuniting of mother and daughter church. Joining hands seemed

Bid Us God Speed

to be a sign of the times. Back in 1948 merger on the national level took place with the joining of the Evangelical and Reformed churches with the Congregational Christian churches to become the United Church of Christ. The successful University of Life cosponsored by First and Edwards continued year after year, while the previous combined church schools had been a benefit to the youngsters of both congregations. Summer services were a joint venture, with each church hosting half of the twelve Sundays.

In 1950 a committee was appointed to study the question of union. This study group was later enlarged to sixty members, thirty representing each church. By 1952 both congregations learned that the committee was in favor of merger. A new building on new land was ruled out because of an estimated cost of at least $500,000. But there was a simple solution. For a sum of $75,000, First Church could be renovated—which, along with the addition of a small chapel for weddings, funerals, and the like—could serve the needs of both churches. The combined congregations would have a total membership of well over one thousand, and the Sunday school would have about four hundred. The new name had a satisfying ring: the Jonathan Edwards Church of Northampton.

If ever these two very independent Congregational churches were to get together, it certainly seemed that there was no better time than the present. The big decision took place on June 3, 1952. First Church overwhelmingly voted for the merger, with 89 percent in favor of it. At Edwards a total of 214 members voted; 140 voted yes and 74 no. Edwards lacked the necessary two-thirds approval by just 3 votes! Edwards drew up the consolidation proposal for reconsideration, and this time the vote passed by the needed two-thirds margin. Merger plans could proceed.

For the final union vote on May 20, 1953, 419 people appeared at the Edwards Church meeting for the crucial decision. All were members, but there were many unfamiliar faces among the regular churchgoers! The vote was a resounding no to accept the "Agreement of Consolidation" and the transfer of property (the average vote on these two questions being 180 yeses and 237 noes). There was another surprise just down the road. First Church recorded 123 votes in favor and 71 votes against in response to all questions, this time lacking the two-thirds votes needed for the merger.

Sprucing up the Old Church

It was back to square one. Two choices remained for Edwards—restore or rebuild. Basic repairs would come to $25,000, while extensive alterations would total $244,000. Estimates for building a new church on a new site ranged from $250,000 to $268,000. Many—certainly a majority—felt that the difference was not all that great and restoration was voted down handily, 191 to 57. In the spring of 1954 a majority vote decided the fate of the old landmark—the decision was a new church on a new site.

Changes seemed to be occurring everywhere. The Reverend Whipple left for Danvers to take up a new pastorate. His stay here was punctuated by postwar concerns for its victims, the communist threat, and cold war, and the proposed church merger. He met these challenges while caring deeply for his congregation. The *Gazette* recalled that

One church member said that, on two occasions, he was no sooner in his hospital bed than Mr. Whipple was on hand as the first caller. And he did not confine his calls to members of his own church. He visited patients of other churches and faiths when he knew them, or heard about them.

1954-1960

Richard Linde

Building the Present Church

ANY BRUISED AND battered feelings seemed to heal quickly under the positive leadership of the new minister, Richard Linde, an idea man who loved a challenge. Building the new Edwards Church would be just that. Mr. Linde held a master's degree in business administration from Harvard as well as a Bachelor of Divinity degree from Drew Theological Seminary. For the moment, he and his family were settling into the new parsonage at 33 Prospect Avenue.

For the coming task, the new minister was assisted by

another newcomer, Thomas Taylor. This likable first-year student at the Boston School of Theology was given charge of religious education. Before the year's end the strength and potential of Edwards Church was very much in evidence. The "Loyalty Dinner" at Smith School was an event not to be forgotten by any of the 411 members present. Led by Dr. Philip Viscidi, chairman of the board of trustees, and by campaign leaders Charles DeRose, Dr. James Cavanagh, and Merrill Torrey, a grand total of $204,047.46 was raised in pledges. The *Gazette* observed that "undoubtedly the most inspired and tireless worker of the entire canvas was Arthur Condon who was . . . a shining example to the entire committee and congregation." Other faithful workers were Paul Graham, Richard Holden, and Dr. LeRoy Ames. Meanwhile, Dr. William Arnold directed the most successful budget drive in the history of the church.

The old high school building site across the street seemed to be an ideal location for the new building, and it was favored by the building committee. For much of 1955, the old high school property became a political hot potato, with most of the juggling going back and forth among the city council, the city property committee, and the school committee. With a clear title in doubt, the church building committee could let no more time slip by. The bid to purchase the property was withdrawn. But there were other sites under consideration. One was a large two-house lot on Elm Street that was an attractive prospect; another was the land on which the old church now stood.

Several experts expressed the opinion that since the present location served the city as a whole and was handy for Smith College students as well, the church should rebuild there. They felt that a church on the Elm Street lot would take on the character of a neighborhood. On December 7, 1955, the members voted to rebuild on the old and familiar corner of State and Main streets, a short two weeks after rejecting the old high school site.

Case closed? Hardly. Powerful arguments for the property on Elm Street—opposite Maynard Road—began to surface. Robert Jordan, chairman of the building committee, believed that this alternative had not been fully considered. Stepping down from the committee, he and a number of other members of the congregation felt that the Elm Street site on Route 9, an attractive and major throughway for the city, was the geographical center of Northampton. The location offered parking aplenty (now

Building the Present Church

Architect's rendering of proposed Elm Street Church.

lacking), and there was room for expansion. The twelve-room adjacent Pollard house needed no renovation and could be used for Christian education or other purposes. Several well-known experts in church building agreed, adding that it would be a shame to rebuild just two blocks from the mother church, which had similar goals and programs.

A petition that resurrected the new church location question was successful, but the church vote on May 16, 1956, was not. Out of 324 voting members, the Elm Street site mustered only 125 votes. Mr. Jordan immediately announced that his group would join the majority, and a unanimous vote made the State Street-Main Street location final. Democracy has always been a cornerstone of the Congregational Church. Every voice was as important as the issues that were involved. In the spirit of Christian brotherhood, with few exceptions, the minority closed ranks with the rest. Edwards Church stood on the threshold of a new exciting future, united in purpose and positive in its direction.

The optimism was contagious. Attendance at Sunday worship rose to 428 in 1956. Edwards had become the eleventh largest Congregational Church in Massachusetts. This large

Bid Us God Speed

body of worshipers would soon be meeting in a church of modern A-frame construction—a decided contrast to Northampton's nineteenth-century downtown area.

Modern architecture aside, there was no less an awareness of the earlier Pilgrim and Puritan heritage. Mr. Linde's eighteenth-century clerical collar was patterned after Jonathan Edwards's own. Before Christmas of 1955 the Sarah Edwards Ring (named for Jonathan's wife), had made Puritan collars for both the carol and the tower children's choirs. In October of that year Jonathan Edwards's 252d birthday was commemorated. Rev. Linde paraphrased Edwards's most famous sermon "Sinners in the hands of an Angry God," comparing the indulgent God people believe in today with the stern God of Edwards. The hymns, written by Jonathan Edwards's contemporaries, were well known to the churchgoers: "O God Our Help in Ages Past" and "Jesus Shall Reign" by the prolific Isaac Watts and "David's Lamentation" by William Billings, who has been called the first American composer.

With the Massachusetts Incorporation Act of 1953, Edwards Church was officially known as "The Jonathan Edwards Church of Northampton, Massachusetts." The Reverend and Mrs. Linde's admiration for our namesake was evidenced well before coming to Northampton when they named their first son Richard Edwards. After moving here, Mrs. Linde gave birth to the first Northampton boy of the New Year in 1956, named Thomas Hooker after the first minister in the Connecticut Valley.

Mr. Linde's sermons were memorable. Here are noted a few of the intriguing titles of his sermons—each carrying a message that was hard to forget: "The Loud Silence," "The Foreign Policy of the Kingdom of God," "The Problem of a little Dishonesty," "Your God is too small," "Why Girls fail in College," "A Life for ten cents," "The Man Who invented Sin," "Blundering into Paradise," and the "How-to-Be" series that included: "How to be Happy," "How to be Good," and "How to be Successful." Like one of the Men's Club's hearty communion breakfasts, they stayed with each churchgoer for a long time.

One of his early series of sermons made the *Gazette* headlines of January 4, 1955: "Minister Wants to know America's Favorite Sins." Mr. Linde had sent out six hundred letters with enclosed postcards to Smith College students, teenagers, church members, fellow clergymen and Northampton businessmen

Building the Present Church

The Carol Choir, November 1956.

—as well as to more than one hundred others across the country. His poll found that the worst evil listed was youth delinquency, followed in order by alcoholism, drug abuse, political corruption, poor racial relations, murder, dishonesty, promiscuous sex, war, and inadequate care of the mentally ill. Lack of courtesy received only 51 votes, while lack of church attendance received but 30. When asked what sin he would pick, Mr. Linde replied, "I'm just against it." His "7 favorite sins" series was eagerly awaited by the congregation—and by the general public through the WHMP broadcasts.

Characteristic of the minister's sense of humor is the following note from the *Spire*. Although not original, it should have given "Shunday" members some food for thought.

Dxar Frixnds:
This typxwirtxt is an xxcxllxent machinx, but it has onx sxrious dfxct. On of thx lxttxers is missing, and handicaps us in our work. Wx arx anxious to usx this machinx, you sxx, but thx absxncx of onx lxttxr provxs vxry xxasprating at timxs bxcausx whxn you nxxd it, it isn't thxrx.
Wx havx somx mxmbxrs absxnt from thx church sxrvicxs. So wx arx writing this notx to txll you that whxn you arxn't thxrx, our church is likx this typwritxr. Wx arx sxriously handicapped by thx absxncx of onx kxy mxmbxr.

Sincxrxly yours,
Richard Linde
Ministxr

There were new directions for the new church at the crossroads of State and Main. An important bylaw change in 1955 created a church council, responsible to the membership, to plan

Bid Us God Speed

the work of the church and to coordinate boards and organizations. Under the church council were the board of directors, board of deacons, board of deaconesses, board of finance, and board of education.

The Reverend Edward C. Bottemiller, fresh from completing two years of graduate study at Yale Divinity School, became the full-time assistant minister in 1957. Joining him on the staff was Mrs. Esther Newhall as director of religious education. She started a Sunday school Lenten giving program to buy a record player for the children's ward at Ryder Memorial Hospital in Puerto Rico. Since the children there spoke little English, a recording of several songs in both English and Spanish was sent along with the player. The primary department sang "I will follow Jesus"; the junior department, "Fairest Lord Jesus."

The following year, the Gideon's Guard project stimulated interest in Bible memory work and religious reading. A Christmas Eve candlelight service involved over one hundred teachers, children, and members of the congregation. By 1960 the Sunday school membership had increased by 50 percent, and church membership reached the nine hundred mark. With the marked increase in attendance, the Butler and Ulman building next door was purchased for school use in 1961. The results of the postwar baby boom were being felt.

The Young People's Fellowship developed new programs. In 1955 the group started the Hamp Canteen at the church on Saturday evenings. Dancing and light refreshments provided a relaxed social setting. On Sunday evenings the group conducted a program of worship, study and recreation. One example was the visit to St. Mary's Church, where Father David P. Welch discussed Catholicism. The next week was a follow-up discussion on "If I Marry a Roman Catholic," with a skit on the same subject. It was a worthwhile step in the appreciation and cooperation between Christians of different faiths. Like discussions were conducted in 1957 as well.

There was an increased emphasis on the family. The fourth Sunday of each month was set aside as Family Sunday when children attended church with their parents. There were field trips for juniors; the high school class went to the Cathedral in the Pines in Rindge, New Hampshire; a retreat was held in the Congregational Center in Framingham, Massachusetts for older young people; a Halloween casserole party, a potluck Christmas dinner, and a Look Park picnic were also among the family

Building the Present Church

The Edwards Church, 1972.

Bid Us God Speed

events. The "Stork Operation" for new mothers brought a meal to the family every night for one week after mother and infant had returned home from the hospital.

These good times in no way conflicted with the Edwards outreach program. In 1958 a new envelope system increased contributions by 33 percent, allowing the church to support several missionaries. The Reverend Kenrick M. Baker, Jr., headed the Fellowship Center and School among French Huguenots. Dr. John A. Smith served as both physician and minister at the Ryder Memorial Hospital in Puerto Rico. Other financial support was sent to Miss Manorama Powar, the Edwards' missionary in India. Locally, funds were supplied to the Hampshire County Sanatorium as well as to Rev. Osmond Billings, a hospital visitor to patients who had no nearby friends and relatives or church.

The year 1958 also marked the 125th anniversary, celebrated, appropriately, in the mother church. As of October 1957 First Church graciously permitted Edwards the use of its facilities while the new building was under construction. Highlighting the celebration was the play *Fortitude,* written by Mrs. Marjorie Cavanagh, depicting the beginning of the church in 1833.

The Christmas Eve candlelight service, long a tradition at Edwards, was made all the more memorable, as it was the first service in the new church! True, John Ebel's hardworking property crew were still returning church possessions from storage, but the sanctuary was ready enough for the great gathering that filled the pews and lined the aisles. As in the past, the Christmas story was told in costume, story, and song. When the pageant was over, the sanctuary was darkened. Only the large central candle representing Christ gave light to the blackness of the night. From this flame of Christ, other candles were lit. Symbolically, His light spread through the congregation as it did throughout the world. And so light did indeed fill the new church, promising an ongoing dedication to the Word of God through his newborn son.

While the Christmas Eve service set the stage for the homecoming of the Edwards congregation, other prededication activities were off and running. "Exuberant" is the word that comes to mind when the young people saw the New Year in. Early in the evening a dinner was enjoyed at the Youth Center, followed by a feature motion picture, *The Fuller Brush Man,* with Red Skelton. A dance followed with streamers, noisemakers,

Building the Present Church

View from the chancel.

Bid Us God Speed

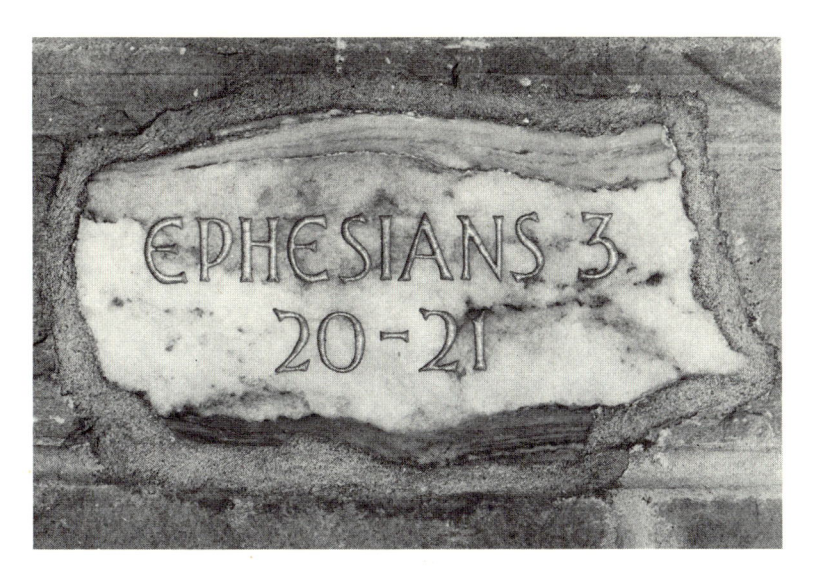

The Dedication Stone.

balloons, and hats. There was certainly a change of pace when the young people attended the half-hour New Year's Eve service with their elders. But they were off again at 12:01 A.M. with a snake dance down Main Street!

On January 4, 1959, the 9:30 A.M. and 11:00 A.M. Sunday services were the first to be held in the new building. Mr. Linde's sermon, quite appropriately, was entitled "Stumbling Over the Cross." The huge Swedish iron cross, not yet hung, was resting in the front aisle of the nave.

The long-awaited Dedication Week opened on February 22 with a special organ prelude by Doric Alviani. Dr. Penner returned to a new pulpit and his old congregation with the sermon, "What is it Worth to You?" (Perhaps he was referring to the $450,000 that made the new church possible.) That afternoon over one thousand Northamptonites toured the new facilities during an open house sponsored by the deaconesses. Visitors found Christian symbolism everywhere. Guests were told that from the South Street approach, the steeply pitched roof and spire suggest hands held in prayer. The great triangular window, with its framed crosses, seems to invite passersby to look at the eighteen-foot lighted cross (no longer a stumbling hazard) in the chancel. Inside the sanctuary, the old Coolidge pew con-

Building the Present Church

Congregational history in stone: the sidewall facing State Street.

trasts with the contemporary interior. The natural stone of the chancel walls represents the rugged New England countryside. The solid white marble communion table, centered in the chancel, was purposely set away from the wall to emphasize the freedom that Congregationalists enjoy when gathering about the Lord's table rather than as worshiping before an altar. To the congregation's left is the lectern of Makassar ebony and Swedish iron with a carving of God's hand clasping that of man. To the right and in the nave wall is the dedication stone of marble from the ancient city of Ephesus, to which the Apostle Paul wrote his New Testament Letter to the Ephesians. The dedication verses are "now to Him who by the power at work within us is able to do far more abundantly than all that we ask or think, to Him be

Bid Us God Speed

glory in the church and in Christ Jesus to all generations, for ever and ever. Amen" (Eph. 3:20-21).

Before returning to the outdoors, members are reminded by the huge "window on the world" of Christ's message to go out and preach the Gospel. On State Street, flanking the base of the stone cross on the side of the building, are four carved stones in relief. To the upper left, the *Mayflower* sails its stone sea to bring the Pilgrims and Congregationalism to Massachusetts. The upper right depicts the likeness of Thomas Hooker, leader of the 1636 migration from the Massachusetts coast to Hartford and the first minister in the Connecticut River Valley. On the lower left is Jonathan Edwards, after whom Edwards Church is named. To the lower right is the "Haystack Prayer Meeting" of 1806 at Williams College. The old church bell, cast in 1871, is displayed in the courtyard. Its inscription reads "Edwards Church built 1833, burnt and rebuilt in 1870." On the other side is "Let Him That Heareth Say Come."

Following a program-filled week and the Sunday service, the cornerstone was laid. Behind it and sealed in a copper case were messages from the builders, architects, the mayor, and church officials. Already in place were the companion stones from old 1833 and 1872 buildings. Edwards was ready to face a new future in its new church.

1960-1975

Richard K. Beebe

The Ecumenical Movement

SIXTY NEW MEMBERS were added during the first four and one half months of the new building's existence. Shortly after Sunday services began in the new sanctuary, 70 percent of the building debt had been paid! Affluence, accomplishment, and enthusiasm were signs of the times in the 1960s. Possessions were within the reach of more people, and having two cars in the garage seemed a reasonable goal for everyone. With the new church on a firm footing, Mr. Linde was off to new challenges at the First Congregational Church of Elyria, Ohio.

About this time, seven local churches of the Northampton Council of Churches exchanged ministers for Sunday services. It was not an earth-shaking idea in itself, but it was a first for our city—and a hint of interchurch cooperation to come. In the spring of 1960 the Reverend Richard K. Beebe, attached to the Board of Home Missions of the Congregational Christian Church, accepted a call as the church's seventeenth pastor. From the start Mr. Beebe became Edwards's goodwill ambassador. Somehow, he seemed to know everyone's name in town! His warm and friendly personality invited a closeness between the various religious groups of the city.

The union summer services, held jointly between Edwards and the First Church, were continued. In 1961 the annual Massachusetts Conference of Congregational Churches met at Edwards in a strong showing of unity. Later the congregation took part in celebrating the mother church's three hundredth anniversary. The annual Reformation Sunday marked the anniversary of Martin Luther's posting of the 95 theses on the Wittenburg University church door in 1517. Some two thousand members of the participating Protestant churches jammed John M. Greene Hall for the event.

For years the Protestant churches had joined to provide released-time religious education outside the public schools. However, transportation problems and "various practical reasons" brought this effort to a close in 1965. But that same year different Protestant denominations sponsored a United Lenten program featuring six seminars at Edwards. Discussions centered around "How and Why We Differ—a Comparison of Protestant Differences," "How and Why of Bible Study," and "The Church in the World." In the fall there was an interchurch educational program held at both Edwards and First Church for junior and senior high school students, while an adult group delved into "Understanding Denominations."

The Protestant churches had closed ranks in a spirit of understanding and cooperation, but what of Edwards's Roman Catholic brothers? Encouraging indeed was the 1960 Ecumenical Week of Prayer for Christianity. This was a revolutionary change, as services of worship were held at both First Church

Bid Us God Speed

and St. Mary's Church. Priests and ministers also met in a series of meetings for Bible study and problems of concern to all Christians. Mr. Beebe explained that "The purposes of any activity on an ecumenical level are to understand each other and to express our Christian unity and solidarity. The purposes are not—on either side—to correct or to conform."

By January 1966 the ecumenical movement was in high gear. There was a service of prayer for the "Unity of Christ's Church" with combined Protestant and Catholic congregations. Because of its success, another such service was held the following year. The Reverend Beebe preached a sermon in which he said that "In the past, we have prayed for Christian unity separately, but tonight we rejoice that we are able to meet and pray for Christian unity together."

Referring to Pope Paul VI's Ecumenical Council that included non-Catholic churchmen, Mr. Beebe said that Vatican II's crowning achievement was the communication and cooperation between faiths. "I think there are certain doors open to us here in this city, if we are eager and willing to enter them!" To back up his words, Mr. Beebe proposed a joint Catholic and Protestant Bible study group plus study groups where Protestants and Catholics alike could learn a few basic facts "about each other's beliefs and practices, thereby removing ignorance and suspicion, misunderstanding and misinformation of which there is too much."

This was no idle suggestion. Four months later, a *Gazette* headline startled its readers with "Reformation Day May be Casualty of Ecumenism." Actually, the committee voted only to study a possible change in the name of the observance, "in the spirit of ecumenism." It was also unanimously voted to conduct a joint meeting with the Catholic churches on Pentecost in May 1967, and that these churches be invited to join the Northampton Council of Churches sometime in the future. In May 1966 more than sixty laymen of different faiths met at First Church for two series of six sermons each.

Although the churches of Northampton were pulling together, the children and their parents seemed to be pulling apart. Young people from the postwar were rebeling against old-fashioned values, and there was the devil to pay. A wave of liberalism and changing moral standards seemed to be eroding the very foundations of Christianity. At the annual church meeting in May 1965 the board of education reported that the church

The Ecumenical Movement

was weak in its offerings for high school and college students, while the Sunday school was expanding and vigorous.

Other programs were floundering. The men's communion breakfasts were discontinued because of lack of interest. Even the time-honored Men's Club had died a quiet death the previous year. In 1966 the Reverend Beebe asked his congregation "Is God Dead?"

The annual meeting that year gave scant cheer. The minister noted the downward trend in new members in all churches for the previous eight years. Edwards was no exception, for the Northampton School for Girls was conducting its own Sunday evening sevices and no longer required church attendance. The Burnham School girls were allowed to attend the new Smith Chapel with the college students; and, as a final blow, services at Edwards conflicted with the schedule of Clarke School for the Deaf. There was certainly less interest in, and response to, church organizations in general. Mr. Beebe added that "The weekend exodus plays a larger part each year" and that "both pastor and people are called to be 'open' to the new, the different, the experimental."

In 1967 the budget fell short of its goal. It was reported that the teams of two deacons each, formed to visit all members of the church, found the effort too time-consuming to be continued. The Women's Fellowship winter meeting was canceled because of poor attendance. Doric Alviani, the man who had given such professionalism, vigor, and variety to our church music, resigned. The two services of worship were cut to one as of April. As Mr. Beebe had said three years earlier, "These are perplexing but challenging days to be a minister simply because you and I are living in a period of transition and turmoil, revolution and reform."

Meanwhile, the turmoil and confusion of the 1960s were by no means local. Authority on all levels—from parents to government—was being questioned. Then in November 1963 the nation was plunged into mourning with the assassination of President John F. Kennedy. To an overflowing attendance at two services, the minister reviewed "this monstrous act of murder—a diabolical deed which has polluted the blood of our nation." He spoke for the congregation when he called for a renewal of fair play and justice. "Now perhaps, for just a brief moment, dispite our grief and sorrow, we of this nation can

Bid Us God Speed

stand together as a nation with a common sorrow and forget that we tear ourselves apart with hostilities."

Strife between races made almost daily news in the *Gazette*. A crusader for black people's rights, Ben Brown, was murdered in 1967 in Jackson, Mississippi. The Massachusetts Conference of the United Church of Christ wrote to the president, the Jackson mayor, and our senators, "expressing our deep concern for justice." One year later, Martin Luther King, Jr., fell, victim of a bigot's bullet. Dr. Albert Penner made it clear to the Massachusetts Council that without giant strides toward a just society "there will be more turmoil and violence and a deeper alienation among our people." Further, "The old America with its long legacy of slavery and human degradation must die if the America Martin Luther King saw in his dream is to become a reality."

Edwards tried to offer programs more relevant to the times. Men and women of the parish heard a speaker discuss the new morality and its implications for adults and youth in such areas as sexual behavior, work, and leisure, war and race relations. In 1965 the church cooperated with five other Protestant groups to present the "Fit to Be Tied" series on Christian love and marriage for high school students.

The following year Edwards Church teenagers presented the drama *A Man Dies*. Opening with "School, adults, religion, What's the Use?" they portrayed the life of Christ in contemporary song, dance, and narration. Standard dress was blue jeans and sweatshirts—and the music, supplied by the local combo, Petrified Flies—ranged from emotional ballads to the wildest rock and roll. It was a Christian message in modern terms—and effective.

What was really needed was a young leader—one of the crowd—who could give guidance without being an authority figure. Enter the Reverend Carl E. Cline, the newly appointed minister of youth and education. Within several months he was leading a series of sermons for high school students. Subjects included "Relating to Others," "College or Living Expenses after High School," "Understanding Moods and How to Respond to Them," "Contemporary Social Problems from a Biblical Perspective," and "Questions Man Asks about God."

In 1967 the play *For Heavens's Sake* gave evidence of the considerable versatility and talent of our high schoolers. Dealing

The Ecumenical Movement

with the issues that faced young people, it was presented two evenings to appreciative audiences. This active Young People's Fellowship visited some fifty homes of Edwards's senior citizens during the year. As the group's popularity increased, the Reverend Cline enlarged it to include youth from six Protestant churches as well as some non churchgoers and those of the Catholic faith. But its success was not without problems. The insecurity of the teenagers encouraged an "in" group that excluded some of the other students. Carl (as everyone knew the Reverend Carl E. Cline) noted with some concern that because of this there was less service to others and more self-service.

One topic discussed was religious attitudes toward war. In this regard, Carl had the strength of his convictions, and many were the times that he stood in vigils against the Vietnam War. Time has sided with his views, and the youth of the church profited by his counsel in chaotic times. As Calvin Coolidge once said, "Little progress can be made merely attempting to repress what is evil. Our great hope lies in developing what is good."

The problem of drug abuse was so widespread that the Northampton churches banded together with the schools in a community program of education on the subject. The earlier ecumenical movement laid the groundwork for such a cooperative effort. Meanwhile, the Protestant Ministers Association sponsored an informal four-week series on sex education for eighty high school students.

On a larger scale, the Massachusetts Conference of the United Church of Christ called for respect and support for the right to act in accord with one's conscience in protesting the war in Vietnam. This was similar to its resolution, passed in 1964, recognizing the right of individuals to protest what they considered to be unjust laws. Carl's efforts here—sometimes unpopular with some in the congregation—had strong support from the member churches of this state.

The spirit of union and cooperation between Protestant churches and the ecumenical spirit in Northampton was ongoing in the 1970s. Perhaps difficult times made the common bond of Christianity all the more important. This joining of hands in the spirit of brotherhood and cooperative strength was not lost on Edwards Church and First Church. By 1975 the combined church school had prospered for seven years. And in spite of the recently built Edwards Church, a merger with the mother con-

Bid Us God Speed

gregation once again became a topic for discussion—so much so, in fact, that five members from both churches were commissioned to explore just such a move in 1973. Meeting weekly for eight months, this intensive study was completed in May 1974. Both churches voted "heavily in favor" of accepting the committee's recommendation of union.

After nearly 150 years of separation, could it be that the two neighboring Congregational churches would combine their resources and energies to counter the turmoil of the past decade? By June an enthusiastic reunion committee was meeting almost weekly with twenty members from each church. Additional subcommittees were added to make a total of sixty reunion members. Over one thousand man-hours were expended in the effort. All legal documents were prepared and ready. Then, almost as an anticlimax, a meeting of information and discussion was held in both churches on February 2, 1975. There were few questions that hadn't already been answered. The final vote on February 9 seemed almost a formality, and a heavy vote in favor was expected. Ninety-six First Church votes registered for an forty against union. No problem there! Meanwhile, Edwards tallied its votes—118 for and 67 against—but not quite the two-thirds majority needed! Somewhat dumbfounded church officials could only despair that less than half of the eligible voters had turned out for this all-important step. A few stay-aways had killed the merger—at least for the near future.

As a result of the vote the Edwards education committee decided to withdraw the church school from the cooperative venture, but "hoped to continue cooperation wherever possible." Edwards now faced a complete rebuilding of its programs and aims—alone. But the future was only one of optimism.

The January Founders Day celebrated the burning of the final mortgage payment—now there would be increased funds available for benevolences and church programs. There was an appreciation of the church's senior members who had helped shape the church's course in years past. Rachel Ashwanden was given special recognition on her retirement as treasurer. Hazel Langdon had just completed fifteen years of dedicated work as church secretary, and she was remembered on her birthday with gratitude. Looking about the congregation, one could see that there were countless other good and faithful parishioners who had unselfishly made both time and money available to their church. With a membership such as this, one could look forward

The Ecumenical Movement

to a whole new era of challenges and achievements without reservation!

Mr. Beebe was retiring at age sixty-five—the first of the many changes to come. In his last report in the annual meeting he wrote:

Just out of curiosity, I checked my Record Books, and this is what I found. Since I began my work as Minister of our church in September 1, 1960
I have baptized 211 children (most of whom take a dim view of Baptism!);
I have conducted 406 funerals (each one takes something out of you);
I have officiated at 179 weddings (A minister knows he's not a young man any more when, as he is performing a wedding, he suddenly realizes that the bride's mother looks better to him than the bride does!)
Between September 1, 1960, and August 31, 1975, I will have preached 555 sermons (Do you remember any of them?)

Always remembered, certainly, will be his outgoing personality and kindly concern—he was a truly dedicated Christian who guided our congregation through some of its most distressing and challenging times.

1975-1979

J. Gregory Tweed

Family Participation and Local Concerns

A NEW MINISTER was to head this renewal of the Edwards spirit—Gregory Tweed. The pastoral search committee found

Greg very likeable, and were drawn to him as a person. . . . He shows a ready concern for and sensitivity to people, and is the sort of

Bid Us God Speed

person who makes a good counsellor. . . . A man of many talents, Greg Tweed is, we believe, a minister who will lead us well in the years ahead.

The Reverend Tweed did, indeed, have many talents. He could draw and sketch (his oil painting of Jonathan Edwards now hangs in the Heritage Room), had a professional singing voice, and was something of a gourmet cook. The *Gazette Hampshire Life* of December 1977, in a profile on the man, said that

Gregory Tweed did not go into politics, as was his original intent, and he also turned off the route to musical superstardom. Yet he does have the drive, and some say the ambition, of a rising politician. He is a dedicated man of the cloth, but he is a complex and interesting a personality as many men whose missions on earth are less clearly revealed.

The committee on planning and review, began under the Reverend Beebe, took on added importance. In the 1977 *Annual Meeting Report* were pages of projected goals, many beginning with such words as "develop," "expand," "add," "increase," "broaden," and "rejuvenate." There was no doubt that changes were on the way.

Perhaps one of the more exciting innovations was the closer contact of the children with the congregation. Margaret Owens, director of the church school, and her assistant, Sandra Rossi, shepherded their flock of kindergartners through the eighth graders through many projects. To climax their study of worldwide Christmas customs, the youngsters held a Christmas dinner for everyone, which included the enthusiastic demolition of a piñata they had made. As a Christmas gift to the congregation, the children gave members a much-appreciated continental breakfast. Yet another contact was the recent and continuing tradition of choosing honorary classmates from the congregation and remembering them with cards and gifts on special occasions. They also helped their elders in the church fair and at food sales. At regular worship services, children representing the Sunday school joined the adult ushers in presenting their offerings. The youngsters will probably never forget the fun of "turn-around Sunday," when their parents attended Sunday school while they took part in the grown-up service!

Family Participation and Local Concerns

Increased junior high school membership made possible a Junior Choir. Young people worked on informal suppers with parental help. Youth Sunday as always involved all the youth of the church in singing and worship. A well-attended family retreat to Cape Cod was spiritually stimulating and fun to boot. The Edwards family—including people of various ages and talents—was working together, in contrast to the generally chaotic 1960s.

Still, the backlash of the previous decade was very much in evidence. Society's misfits—the drug addicts, the alcoholics, the lawbreakers, the emotionally scarred, and the unemployables—found a concerned friend in Mr. Tweed. Although neither a psychiatrist nor a psychologist, Greg Tweed helped rebuilt shattered self-images "with practical, loving advice." His "street ministry" became something of a one-man crusade.

This concern for the problems of local people did not go unnoticed by the Christian outreach committee. There was renewed involvement in home missionary efforts as emphasized by the earlier pastor, Rev. Gordon Hall, and now by Tweed. The idea that "charity begins at home" was evident in the 1979 contributions. Recipients were the Northampton Area Council of Churches, the Hampshire United Way, the Pastoral Counselling Service, the Protestant Youth Center of Western Massachusetts, as well as the Bureau for Exceptional Children of Western Massachusetts.

Financial aid was also given to more distant missions, including the Danslan Research Center (dedicated to the improvement of relations between the Muslims and the Christians in the Philippines), Charles Hall Youth Services (American Indian), Scott-Morgan Habitat (Appalachian Mission), CARE and the Heifer projects (to fight world hunger), as well as special collections for the Cambodian Hunger Relief and for "One Great Hour of Sharing." What of the decades of giving to the Ryder Memorial Hospital in Puerto Rico? In 1966 the special Christmas collection was not used for equipment as expected; and there was no response to our letters as to who would replace our missionaries, Dr. John and Virginia Smith. Following the will of the congregation, local charities became the beneficiaries of this sizable sum formerly given to Ryder.

After four brief but colorful years with Edwards Church, the Reverend Tweed returned to his native New York as minister at the Fort Washington Collegiate Church. With his help, the old

Bid Us God Speed

Edwards Church family spirit had weathered some very difficult times.

1979-

Anthony E. Acheson

A Church for All Ages

THE REVEREND ANTHONY E. ACHESON became the nineteenth minister in October 1979, although his formal installation was not held until January of the following year. Behind him was his theological training at the Episcopal Divinity School of Cambridge and his experience as associate minister in Hamilton, Ohio. Ahead was the leadership of Edwards Church, now nearly 150 years old.

Edwards continued to contribute to the Christian way of life—and not the least was its ongoing emphasis on local missionary works. This was the year that the Northampton Survival Center had its start—a place where food and clothing could be obtained by the needy. Each cooperating church was assigned a regular collection Sunday, and few of the congregation at Edwards passed by the large barrel in the rear of the sanctuary without adding to the pile.

Other new area missions appeared in the Christian outreach report such as Respite Care (working with elderly care-givers), the Companion Program (special program for youth and others), the Radio Ministry, Salvation Army work in the Northampton area, *These Days* (outreach literature), Parents Anonymous (child abuse), the Honor Court (a service group of reformed alcoholics), and the American Red Cross for local disaster relief.

The children were back in the news celebrating the two hundredth anniversary of Sunday schools in 1980. Included was a recognition of their teachers, a dedicated and innovative group of volunteers. At the traditional reenactment of the First Thanksgiving Service sponsored by area churches, Edwards sent ten "Pilgrims," one "Indian," and "Elder Brewster."

At Christmas time there were three evenings of Advent worship services preceded by suppers and other activities. Traveling carolers gave presents of shells to church members in nursing homes. A vesper service featured the church school's play, *Little Stars of Bethlehem*. Animals helped in the singing of "The Friendly Beasts," and a tableau with music depicted the nativity scene. The Lenten season featured the school theme, "Have You Ever Been Hungry?" The joy of sharing was emphasized by food offerings to the Survival Center. The children also presented palms to the congregation. Such are but a few examples of how the youngsters have been a very real part of their church—and how they have learned about the importance of helping others.

For the youth group, there were intriguing programs that would interest any of their elders. They did a "roving reporter" study for Advent called "What does Christmas Mean to You?" Random interviews were held at various shopping areas and homes where people of different ethnic backgrounds described their Christmas memories. They also found time to present a play at Christmas vespers. After the holiday season they explored the subject of "Death and Dying" in a series of talks and discussions. Included were speakers who described the medical changes when death occurs and who explored the question of immortality. There was even a field trip to Dutton's Funeral Home. They tried awareness exercises, offered a mini-fair and a breakfast, and took a three-day trip to New York City.

Under the leadership of Carol Taylor, the youth group was now known as TEAM (The Edwards Ageless Ministry). "We have shown," said the director, "that a youth ministry is youth and adults working together at being the church. It is discovery, caring, growing in faith and love."

Children and the youth of the church were growing in numbers and in awareness of service to others. What about the adults? Although membership has decreased slightly over the past ten years, dedication to the church family seems definitely on the upswing. For example, the loyalty Sunday committee reported to the 1981 annual meeting that pledging support had increased dramatically for the fourth successive year. For 1981 approximately $66,000 was raised—an all-time high. A stewardship committee was formed to insure the financial health of the church, the better to fulfill its Christian mission. Its parent organization, the committee on planning and review, continued to reevaluate old programs and to establish guidelines for those

Bid Us God Speed

in the future. The importance of such overall planning cannot be overestimated.

Such positive action should help the church grow in numbers. Meanwhile, Tony Acheson hit upon a novel way to increase the membership of Edwards. On August 7, 1982, he took as his bride Nancy Riege of Hartford. The church school may also benefit by such forward thinking!

One hundred and fifty years have passed since the Reverend John Todd came by stagecoach to lead the newly formed Edwards Society. The mother church was not forgotten, and close ties and cooperation have continued through these many years. Nineteen ministers have led the congregation during good times and bad. Through it all, a flexible and energetic Edwards Church family has emphasized local and worldwide missions, fine music, relevant programs, and service to others.

On this anniversary it may be appropriate to reevaluate the direction our church is taking today. History has shown that we are influenced by the time in which we live. It also has shown that those who have well defined plans are able to shape our destiny. Does this church know where it wants to be in spiritual growth and outreach in five years? In twenty years? What has it learned, for instance, from the many attempts to re-unite with the mother church? Has this building gradually become, for some of us, the church?

The traditions of Congregationalism encourage differences, dissent, and individualism but Christianity has always tempered these human contradictions with charity, kindness, and love. A Christian democratic congregation, therefore, works in a spirit of cooperation to carry out the programs and decisions of the church in the best way possible, but there must be no compromise in its unswerving dedication to its main purpose. Every action of the church should relate to it, grow out of it, and further it.

The questions each member must ask are these: What *is* the fundamental basic thrust of Edwards? What is she now? What does she want to become?

Finding these answers and acting on them will be an exciting challenge to every member.

A Church for All Ages

"We are a Church!

We are a church—a community, a family of the people of God; a place where people can come for the nurturance, support and mutual sharing that are essential to the religious life; an organization whose members can accomplish so much more collectively than individually. Important as finances are—we are not a business. Important as human relationships are—we are not a social club. Important as ethics are—we are not a charitable organization. We are a church!
The questions which concern my ministry are fundamental to our purpose. Are we growing as spiritual beings and as fully human beings? Are we growing in love for ourselves, for people we know, for those we will never know? In short, are we growing in our love for God, and are we willing to act in such a way that we become instruments of His? We are a church. This is what we are about. As we look to the future, let us be about it.

Anthony E. Acheson

Bid Us God Speed

THE EDWARDS CHURCH FAMILY ALBUM

a photographic selection

The Rev. John Todd, 1800-1873.

Mrs. William H. Stoddard, first Directress of the Edwards Church Auxiliary of the W.B.M., circa 1865.

The Rev. Gordon Hall, 1823-1879.

"Cap'n" Enos Parsons in his law office in 1872.

Group photo of Edwards Church friends, taken to give to Mary Daniels before she went to Japan, circa 1887-88.
First row: Mrs. Couring, Mrs. Kneeland, Mollie Kneeland, Clara Clark
Second row: Ella Clark, Annie Bridgman, Helen Lincoln, Mollie Clark, Clara Bodman, Mina Wood
Third row: Miss Kneeland, Carrie Lincoln, Alice Clark, Lizzie Bradford

Members of the Rev. Isaac Clark, Kneeland, Bridgman, and Bodman families on July 4, 1891.

Family Album

"The Wonderful Peck Family," a doll show at the Edwards Church, March, 1893.
First row: (floor) Julia Hartwell, Miss Atkinson of Japan
Second row: (seated) Harry Crafts, Gertrude Brewster, Frank Sheldon
Third row: (standing) Charles Marshall, C. H. Tucker, C. M. Clark, Laura Kidder, Matie Smith, Robert Weir, Norman Brainerd

Church interior, 1898.

Pageant at the First Church 275th Anniversary celebration on June 7, 1936 reenacted the presentation of the silver service to the Edwards Church in 1834.
Left to right: H. E. Wells, R. E. Reynolds, the Rev. Ray Gibbons, the Rev. Albert Penner, Earle Parsons, Mabel Russell, Alice Cook, C. H. Lyman, Mabel Pelton, Helen Crittenden, W. H. Wilson

Clara P. Bodman cuts the cake at the 105th Anniversary of the Edwards Church on February 5, 1938.
First row: Ruth Ann Belding, John Belding, Clara Bodman
Second row: Robert Belding, Lucia Smith Belding, Albert Penner, Joyce Belding, C. H. Lyman

Family Album

The Carol Choir, just before Christmas, 1954.
Cindy Brown (with wreath), John Antil, Pamela Hazenzahl, Peggy Hazenzahl, Anne Jordan, David Swift, Joseph Adams

Choir members light candles on December 23, 1954.
Niles Jacoby, Julie Cavanagh, Mary Lou Addison, Peter DeRose

The Carol Choir, 1955.

Family Album   81

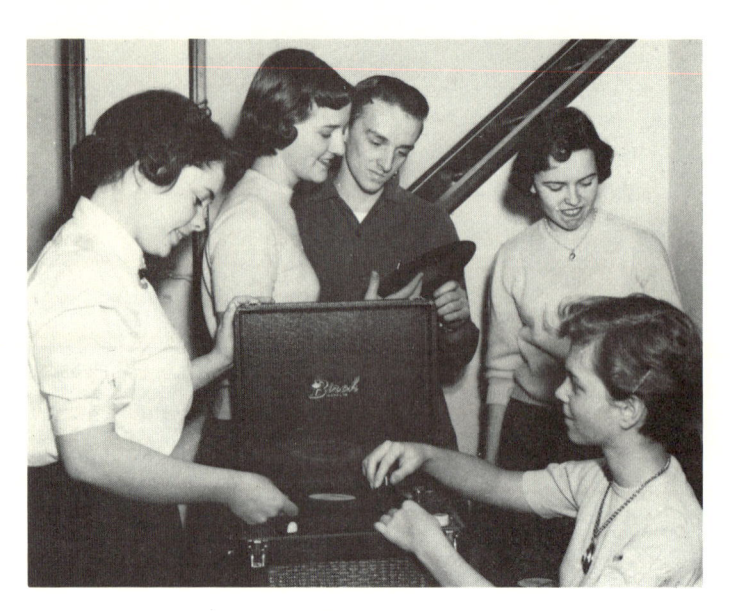

The Edwards Teen Canteen, 1955.
Sabra Sullivan, Judy King, Niles Jacoby, Jean Campbell, Jane Morrison

100th birthday party for Vina Lou Bement with the Rev. Richard Linde, Janet Foster, and Florence Arnold helping to celebrate.

Bid Us God Speed

Demolition, 1957.

Sunday school group, 1957.
Jeffery Brown, Gerry Miller, Meredith Johnston, Susan Cook, Robert Hayden, Judy Arnold

Young Couples Club, November 24, 1957.
Ronald Richan, Bernard Heavey, Joan Metcalfe, Mikkel Kroll, Herbert Hazenzahl, Charles Dutton, Barbara Hibbard, Joseph Brackett, Robert Jordan, Elizabeth Ebel, John Hibbard, Charles Branch, Keith Wilbur. At piano, Ruth Wilbur.

The Tower Choir, 1957-58.
First row: Cynthia Ullman, Meredith Johnston, Sharron Myers, Linda Sue Plumb, Wendy Butler
Second row: Sandra Reuther, Cheryl Smith, Barbara Jordan, Pamela Hazenzahl, Peggy Hazenzahl, Carol Graves, Pamela Arnold, Susan Jordan.

125th Anniversary Pageant "Fortitude," Edwards Church, February 7, 1958.
First row: Kathleen Lord, Lillian Ross, Ethel Swift, Shauneen Kroll, David Jordan, Sharon Ryder
Second row: Obed Rogers, Lester Brooks, Edward Corell, David Jack, Bernard Heavey, Leroy Ames

Family Album

The Chancel Choir, April 2, 1958.

First row: Shauneen Kroll, Ruth Stearns, Doris Holden, Dorothy Ladd, Priscilla Graham, Mabel Gray, Florence Ames, Nancy Hildenbrandt
Second row: Doric Alviani, James Ross, Robert Ames, Ernest Premo, Leroy Ames, Glenn Biggam

Christmas Eve Pageant, 1958.

First row: (floor) George Snook, Stephen Erikson, Stephen Brackett, George Brooks
Second row: (standing) David Wilbur, Roy Gutfinski, Mark Arnold, Paul Graham, Dwight Lee, Sue Jordan, Peter Erikson, Robert Hardy, David Zapata, Chester Allenchey, Lester Brooks

Bid Us God Speed

Dedication dinner, February 27, 1959.

The Rev. Richard Linde, Mrs. Fred Hoskins, John Coolidge, Marjorie Cavanagh, Harold Waggoner (architect), James Cavanagh, Rose Viscidi, Fred Hoskins (speaker), Paul Graham, Florence Coolidge, Philip Viscidi, Sally Kroll, the Rev. John Shaw

The Interpretive Choir, 1966.

First row: Diana Hambley, Donna Kapitan, Marjorie Snedden, Pamela Caldwell, Linda Lenkowski
Second row: Susan Cook, Leigh Erikson, Diane Allenchey

Family Album

The Rev. Richard K. Beebe and Franklin King III examine the 1870 bell, January, 1973.

Committee making Christmas decorations for the Fair, October, 1977.
Joan Tourigny, Elsie Nielsen, Lillian Ross, Nellie Jordan, Marion Phillips

The potato prints appearing here and on pages 69, 70, 71 and 72 were made by Sunday school children as a Christmas gift to church members in 1981.

Family Album

Illustrations and Credits

In the following, the illustrations which appear throughout the text and those in the "Family Album" are listed in the order in which they appear. The abbreviated caption of each is followed by the source, the photographer or delineator where known, and the page on which it appears.

The stylized bust of Jonathan Edwards used on the jacket and elsewhere within the volume was carved in wood by C. Keith Wilbur and photographed by Craig A. Morris. The steel engraving of Warner's Coffee House in 1835 used on the jacket, which shows the First Church at the extreme left and the Edwards Church at the extreme right, was drawn by W. H. Bartlett and engraved by R. Sands. The steel engraving which decorates the endleaves was drawn by James Warner Barber and engraved by S. E. Brown. Both were used through the courtesy of the Northampton Historical Society.

In the credits which follow, the archives of the Edwards Church, source of the majority of the illustrations included, are abbreviated ECA.

Broadside to the congregation, 1832 / ECA / 3
The Edwards Church, 1860 / ECA / 4
Broadside advertising sale of pews / ECA / 6
Communion silver presented 1834 / Photo by Stan Scherer / 7
Temperance Card, 1850 / Northampton Historical Society / 12
After the fire of 1870 / Northampton Historical Society / 16
The second Edwards Church in the early 1900s / ECA / 18
Awards of Merit / Northampton Historical Society / 20
Sunday Toys / *Americana*, Nov. 1973 / 22
Christmas greetings, 1917 / ECA / 30
Calvin and Grace Coolidge / Northampton Historical Society / 32
Rev. Dr. Albert J. Penner / ECA / 36
Whipple family Christmas card / ECA / 44
Proposed Elm Street Church / Courtesy Robert Jordan / 50
Carol Choir, 1956 / ECA / 52
The Edwards Church, 1972 / ECA / Photo by dick fish co., inc. / 54
View from the chancel / ECA / 56
Dedication Stone / ECA / Photo by Stan Sherer / 57
The stone carvings / ECA / Photo by Stanley Sherer / 58
The Rev. John Todd / ECA / 74
Mrs. William H. Stoddard / ECA / 75
The Rev. Gordon Hall / ECA / 76
"Cap'n" Enos Parsons / ECA / 76
Group photo of Edwards Church Friends / ECA / 77
Picnic, July 4, 1891 / ECA / 77
Doll Show at Edwards Church, 1893 / ECA / 78
Church interior, 1898 / ECA / 78
Pageant at First Church, 1936 / ECA / 79
105th Anniversary of Edwards Church, 1938 / ECA / 79
The Carol Choir, December, 1954 / ECA / 80
Lighting candles, December, 1954 / ECA / 81
The Carol Choir, 1955 / ECA / 81
Edwards Teen Canteen, 1955 / ECA / 82
Vina Lou Bement's 100th Birthday / ECA / 82
Demolition, 1957 / ECA / 83
Sunday school, 1957 / ECA / 84
Young Couples Club, 1957 / ECA / 84
Tower Choir, 1957-58 / ECA / 85
125th Anniversary Pageant, 1958 / ECA / 85
The Chancel Choir, 1958 / ECA / 86
Christmas Pageant, 1958 / Courtesy Nellie Jordan / 86
Dedication dinner, 1959 / ECA / 87
The Interpretive Choir, 1966 / Courtesy Esther Newhall / 87
The 1870 bell, 1973 / ECA / 88
Committee making Christmas decorations for the Fair, 1977 / ECA / 89

Index

Abels, Asahel 9
Acheson, Anthony E. 69-72; Increasing membership 70, 71; Marriage 71; "We Are A Church!" 72
Adams, Charles F. 34; Joseph, illus. 80
Addison, Mary Lou, illus. 81
"Agreement of Consolidation" 47
Allenchy, Chester, illus. 86; Diane, illus. 87
Aloha Guild 29, 35
Aloha Mission Circle 35
Alviani, Doric 44, 57, 62, illus. 86
Ames, Florence, illus. 86; Robert, illus. 86
Anderson, Robert 44
Anniversary, Seventy-fifth 27; One hundredth 35; One hundred twenty-fifth 55, 57
Anthony, Susan B. 31
Antil, John, illus. 80
Appalachian Mission 68
Armstrong, James N. 33, 34
Arnold, Florence, illus. 82; Judy, illus. 84; Mark, illus. 86; William 49
Ashwanden, Rachel 65
Atkinson, Miss, illus. 78

Baker, Kendrick M., Jr. 53
Ballard, Clifford 31
Bean, George 45
Beebe, Richard K. 59, 60, 61, 62, 66, 67, illus. 88; Goodwill ambassador 60; Christian unity 60; "Is God Dead?" sermon 61
Belding, John, illus. 79; Joyce, illus. 79; Lucia Smith, illus. 79; Robert, illus. 79; Ruth Ann, illus. 79
Bement, Vina Lou, illus. 82
Biggam, Glenn, illus. 86
Billings, Osmond 55; William 51
Bingham, Clara R. 36; Minerva B. 36
Board of home missions 60
Bodman, Clara, illus. 77, illus. 79; Luther and Philena 43; family, illus. 77
Bottemiller, Edward 53
Branch, Charles, illus. 84
Brackett, Joseph, illus. 84; Steven, illus. 86
Bradford, Lizzie, illus. 77
Brainard, Norman, illus. 78
Brenton, Cranston 28
Brewster, Gertrude, illus. 78; Elder 69
Bridgman, Annie, illus. 77; family, illus. 77
Brooks, George, illus. 86; Lester, illus. 85, 86
Brown, Ben 63; Cindy, illus. 80; Jeffery, illus. 84
Butler, Wendy, illus. 85; Willis H. 26

Caldwell, Pamela, illus. 87
Campbell, Jean, illus. 82
Carol Choir, illus. 52, 81
Cavanagh, James 49, illus. 87; Julie, illus. 81; Marjorie 55, illus. 87
Chancel, view from, illus. 56

Choir, adult 37
Choral Union 37, 38
Christian Endeavorers 29
Christmas, Carols 38, 70; Customs 67; Eve candlelight service 55, 57; Dinner by church schools 67; Greetings, World War I, illus. 30; Pageant 31, 55; Victorian 21
Church council 53
Church school, Edwards 3, 8, 14, 21, 29, 33, 34, 39, 45, 47, 53, 65, 67, 69, 79, 71
Cable, George W., 26
Clark, Alice, illus. 77; C.M., illus. 78; Clara, illus. 77; Donald 31; Ella, illus. 77; Enos 8; family, illus. 77; Isaac 19, 20, 22, 27; Mollie, illus. 77
Clarke, Christopher 5, 9, 27
Clay, Henry 7
Cline, Carl E. 63, 64
Congregational church school 33, 34, 39
Congregational history in stone, illus. 58
Cook, Alice, illus. 79; Benjamin 20; Susan, illus. 84, 87
Coolidge, Calvin 32, illus. 32, 33, 34, 35, 64; Florence, illus. 87; Grace, illus. 32, 34, 35; John 34, 35, illus. 87
Corell, Edward, illus. 85
Couring, Mrs., illus. 77
Crafts, Harry, illus. 78
Crittenden, Helen, illus. 79

Damon, Shirley 45
Daniels, Mary B. 37
Day, George E. 11, 12, 13
Dedication stone, illus. 57, 58, 59
DeRose, Charles, 49; Cora 46; Peter, illus. 81
Dieter, Margaret A. 37
Duryea, Charles 24
Dutton, Charles, illus. 84
Dyer, Lora G. 37

Ebel, Elizabeth, illus. 84; John 55
Edwards Church vii
Edwards Church buildings
1833
    Appearance 4, 5, 6; Burned 1870 16; illus. 16; Dedication 4; Location 4; Pews 5
1872
    Building 16, 17; Interior illus. 18, illus. 78; Remodeling 45; Vote to demolish 48
1958
    Building site alternatives 49, 50; Construction 55; First service 55, 57; Interior 57, 58
Edwards, Jonathan vi, 7, 12, 35, 51; painting of 67, illus. 58; Sarah 51; stone carving 59
Edwards Service Circle 35
Edwards Shop 46
Edwards Society 1, 2, 71
Ellis, Clara E.

Elm Street building site 49, illus. 50
Elm Street parsonage 14, 15
Ely, Joseph B. 34
Erickson, Lee, illus. 88; Peter, illus. 86; Steven, illus. 86

First Church 1, 5, 6, 8, 17, 33, 39, 55, 64, 65; 300th anniversary 60
Fit to be Tied, play 63
For Heavens Sake, play 63
Fortitude, play 55
Foster, Janet, illus. 82
Founders' Day 65
Fund raising 45, 46, 57, 59

Gere, E.O. 25; Henry 5; Henry S. and Martha 20
Gibbons, Ray 39, 40, illus. 79
Goodspeed, F.L. 26
Graham, Paul 49, illus. 86, 87; Priscilla, illus. 86; Sylvester 9
Graves, Carol, illus. 85
Gray, Mabel, illus. 86
Greene, John M., hall 60
Gutfinski, Roy, illus. 86

Hall, Gordon, Sr. 13; Gordon 3, 13, 17, 20, 68, illus. 76; Appearance 14; Civil War sermon 15-16; Family 14; Gift of home 14, 15; Missionary movement 14
Hambley, Diana, illus. 87
Harlow, Marion S. 37; S. Ralph 37
Hardy, Robert, illus. 86
Harris, Gertrude 37
Hartwell, Julia, illus. 78
Hasenzahl, Herbert, illus. 89; Pamela, illus. 80, 85; Peggy, illus. 80, 85
Hayden, Robert, illus. 84
Haystack Meeting stone carving, illus. 58, 59
Heavy, Bernard, illus. 84, 85
Hibbard, John, illus. 84
Hibben, James 8
Hildebrandt, Nancy, illus. 86
Holden, Doris, illus. 86; Richard 49
Home Missionary Society 28, 30
Hooker, Thomas, stone carving, illus. 58, 59
Hoover, Herbert 34
Hoskins, Fred, illus. 87; Mrs. Fred, illus. 87
Hughes, Charles Evans 34

Jack, David, illus. 85
Jacoby, Niles, illus. 81, illus. 82
Johnston, Meridith, illus. 84, 85
Jonathan Edwards Church of Northampton 47, 51
Jones, William 20
Jordan, Anne illus. 80; Barbara illus. 85; David illus. 85; Nellie illus. 89; Robert 49, 50, illus. 84; Susan, illus. 85, 86
Junior Mission Auxiliary 23

Kapitan, Donna, illus. 87
Kennedy, John F. 62
Kidder, Laura, illus. 78
King, Franklin III, illus. 88; Judy, illus. 82
Kneeland, family, illus. 77; Miss, illus. 77; Mrs., illus. 77; Mollie, illus. 77
Kroll, Mikkel 44, illus. 84; Sally, illus. 87; Shauneen, illus. 85, 86

Ladd, Dorothy, illus. 86
Langdon, Hazel 65
Ladies Home Missionary Society 19, 23
Ladies' Prayer Meeting 23
Lee, Dwight, illus. 86
Lenkowski, Linda, illus. 87
Lewis, Margaret 13
Lincoln, Abraham 15, 16; Carrie, illus. 77; Helen, illus. 77
Linde, Richard 48, 49, illus. 82, 87; Building Edwards' third church 51; Our Pilgrim heritage 51; Outstanding sermons 51, 52, 53
Linde, Richard Edwards 51; Thomas Hooker 51
Little Stars of Bethlehem, play 70
Lord, Kathleen, illus. 85
Lucia, Victor N. 28
Lyman, C.H., illus. 79

Market Street parsonage 4
Marshall, Charles, illus. 78
Martin, Luther 60
Martin Luther King, Jr. 63
Mather, Sarah A. 36
Mayflower stone carving 59, illus. 58
Maurer, Irving, war commencement prayer 30, 31
McClurkin, Paul T., Last sermon 42; Letters to servicemen 40, 41, 42; Resignation 42; World War II problems 39
McMillan, Peter 24
Men's club 23, 26, 35, 62
Metcalf, Joan, illus. 84
Middlefield "Den" retreat 45
Miller, Gerry, illus., 84
Mission Study class 30
Missionary Circles and Society 19, 23
Missionary movement 14, 18, 36, 37, 68
Missions, foreign 14, 18, 36, 37, 53
Missions, home 28, 29, 36, 68, 69
Mitchell, John 8, 9, 10; Mrs. John 10
Morrison, Jane, illus. 82
Mother's Club 46
Music 5, 6, 9, 27, 35, 37, 38, 40, 43, 44, 51, 53, 62, 68, 70
Music fund 25
Myers, Sharon, illus. 85

Napier, Thomas 8
Newhall, Esther 53
New Year's celebration 55, 56
Nielson, Elsie, illus. 89

Olson, Raymond 44
Organ 6, 16, 17, 43, 44
Owens, Margaret 67

Parsonages, Crescent Street 31; Elm Street 14, 15; Market Street 4; Paradise Road 24; Prospect Avenue 48
Parsons, Earle, illus. 79; Ellen C. 36; Enos, illus. 76; Mrs. Earl 45; Virginia 45
Pastoral Counselling Service 68
Pelton, Mabel, illus. 79
Penner, Albert J. 35, illus. 36, 63, 79
Phillips, Marion, illus. 89
Plumb, Linda Sue, illus. 85
Pollard house 50
Pope Paul VI 61
Powar, Manorama 55
Premo, Ernest, illus. 86

Ray, George 44
Repairs and remodeling 45, 46, 47, 48
Reusser, Verdi L. 37, 38
Reuther, Sandra, illus. 85
Reynolds, R.E., illus. 79
Richan, Ronald, illus. 84
Riege, Nancy 71
Rogers, E.P. 10, 11
Rogers, Obed, illus. 85
Roosevelt, Franklin and Eleanor 34
Ross, James, illus. 86; Lillian, illus. 89
Rossi, Sandra 67
Russell, Mabel, illus. 79
Ryder, Sharon, illus. 85

Scouting 35, 44
Seelye, Clarke 27
Shaw, John, illus. 87
"Singable Supper" 37, 38
Smith, Cheryl, illus. 85; John A. 55, 68; Matie, illus. 78
Snedden, Marjorie, illus. 87
Snook, George, illus. 86
Social action committee 38
Soldiers' letters, World War II 41, 42
"Spire" 39, 41, 45, 46, 52
Sterns, Ruth, illus. 86
Stimson, Henry L. 34
Stoddard, Sophia H. 36; William H. 8; Mrs. William H., illus. 75
Stone, Harlan F. 34
Suffragettes 28, 31
Sullivan, Sabra, illus. 82
"Sunday toys" 21, 22, illus. 22

Swift, David, illus. 80; Ethel, illus. 85
Symbolism, Edwards Church 57, 58, 59

Taylor, Carol 70; Thomas 49
The Edwards Ageless Ministry (team) 70
"These Days" 69
Three County Fair restaurant 45
Todd, John 1-8, 26, 71, illus. 74
Tomlinson, Ethel 37
Torrey, Merrill 49
Tourigny, Joan, illus. 89
Tucker, C.H., illus. 78
"Turn-around" Sunday 67
Tweed, J. Gregory 66-68

Ullman, Sandra, illus. 85
Union with First Church 33, 39, 40, 46, 47, 64
United Lenten program 60

Van Dyke, Paul 23, 24
Viscidi, Philip 49, illus. 87; Rose, illus. 87

Waggoner, Harold, illus. 87
Weatherall, James 15
Weir, Robert, illus. 78
Welch, David P. 53
Welle-Kum-In Club 32
Welles, Kenneth B. 31
Wells, H.E., illus. 79
Whipple family Christmas card, illus. 44
Whipple, L. Byron 42, 43, 45, 48
Whitney, Josiah 8
Wilbur, C. Keith, illus. 84; David W., illus. 86; Ruth E., illus. 84
Wilson, Woodrow 26
Women's Board of Missions 19
Women's Christian Temperance Union 23, 29
Wood, Henry 31; Irving 37; Katherine H. 36; Mina, illus. 77
Wright, Florence B. 36; Richard 44

Young Ladies' Mission Circle 19, 35
Young People 61, 62, 63, 64, 70
Young People's Fellowship 45, 53, 55, 56
Young People's Forum activities 45
Young People's Missionary Society 19
Young People's Society of Christian Endeavor 23

Zapata, David, illus. 86

Index

The central part of

as drawn by J.W. Barber

The First Congregational Church